ABOVE THE WATERLINE

The Domestic Solid Fuel Boiler

We installed central heating, and built a boiler house outside
We'd taken manufactured solid fuel to test the boiler with pride
He said he'd burn the coal from the pile, we were mystified
It's a boiler for solid fuel, no coal we almost cried.

He was determined to use it, against our good advice
It was burning all right, till he lifted the lid – and surprise
The flame ignited the gas, and burnt his hair and round his eyes
We warned you about your actions and what would arise.

The Domestic Solid Fuel Boiler

I remember a good example of someone who did not heed the good advice given to him on the manufacturer's instructions. It concerned the heating job that was quite a large domestic job run by solid fuel.

This boiler was housed in a boiler house we had built outside. We had filled the system, checked all the joints for leaks and fired the boiler. Now it was going very well on some manufactured fuel we had taken along for the sole purpose of testing it when the customer arrived.

We explained to him that he must use the correct fuel, to which he replied, "Yes I know, but it hasn't arrived yet, so I am going to use coal till it does."

Well, some people tread where angels wouldn't and this was the course he was taking, despite repeated warnings.We retreated whilst he loaded up with coal.

"You'll be sorry."

"It will be all right," he said, grinning all over his face.

Some while after, he went again to the boiler which was top fed, saying, "I'll just see how it's getting on."

As he foolishly lifted the lid, a puff of smoke rose from the open top, which of course was gas.

"It seems to be going all right," he said.

Then whoosh!!! A lick of flame had ignited the gas and before he could jump back it had taken his hair with it. The moral to that is, 'if you won't be ruled, you must be bloody fooled'.

There are, of course, some solid fuel appliances that run on coal and these are very, very good indeed. The coal industries, like the gas and oil industries, protect their customers by insisting that all installers have passed their laid down standards and are members of their particular scheme – what an excellent idea.

But then you can't please everyone. You still get to know all the ones who usually turn out to know nothing. To some you can explain something genuine and it's taken as such, and others think you trying to make them have things they don't want or need. But, for all that, I'm still convinced that honesty is the best policy and it is definitely the only way to gain a good reputation.

Industrial Water Softener

The industrial softener, large and green
I'm going inside, which I'd never seen
They'll feed me in, I wasn't keen
And when you're in, you won't be clean.

Encapsulated inside this softener like lung
Cleaning out gravel and chipping away at the gung
The gravel renewed and from it filtered soft water sprung
To make the bread of life, for old and young.

Industrial Water Softener

There was a large bakery where, from time to time, we did maintenance work and in one room was an industrial water softener. This particular softener stood about six to seven feet high and was three feet in diameter and a manhole was situated some six inches down from the domed top and held in place by two large nuts. Periodically this softener was cleaned out. This meant that someone had to go inside to shovel out the various gravels and, having exposed a filter, chip away the corrosion and clean the pipework.

The powers decided that I should be the one to enter the softener. I was never told who did it before and I still do not know. All the water valves in the softener were closed and everything was drained out, then the two large nuts were removed. The lid was raised up to reveal an oval shaped hole. An electric lead lamp was rigged up and I was told to stand to attention, arms flat against the side of my body to make myself rigid. This I did. I was then picked up and fed through the oval orifice into the softener. It is a good job I do not suffer from claustrophobia. I then, with the aid of a small shovel and electric lead lamp, proceeded to clean out the gravel until it was all removed. By this time I was able to stand upright. As I said, I do not suffer from claustrophobia, but I used to have some terrible thoughts about my body swelling up and not being able to get back out of the hole. One of the reasons I thought like this was probably because of the heat inside the hole, not only from one's own body but also from the electric lead lamp. After a very short time you became wet through with sweat.

It did not help matters when the lads on the outside said, "We are going to put the lid on now, see you later," and then proceeded to slide the manhole cover over the hole.

It is a good thing that I am not subject to a lot of panic but, even though they removed it straight away, the things you imagine could happen or how you could die are unbelievable.

The next thing to happen was that I was sent out with a plumber who turned out to be brilliant at his job. Not only that, he had talent in his feet for he was a very good footballer. If times have changed from those in which football managers are said to have shouted down mineshafts and footballers have appeared, then I suggest they shout within the building trade. Take certain managers of football teams – in particular, a brilliant bricklayer and also a certain former international footballer who is an outstanding plumber. My apologies to the many I have missed, but you are doing a grand job lads.

The Song

I had a boy soprano voice
And when I started work
The lads heard by voice of word
That I could sing, they'd never heard.

By voice of word
They'd never heard
But they'd never leave it there
And wouldn't until they had heard.

Till they had heard
That's all I got
They finally worked out a plot
Sing down the pipes, that was my lot.

Sing down the pipes
I sang the lot
To a shop full of people
They'd worked their plot.

They'd worked their plot
For days I dare not face that lot
They all kept saying, "Oh! What rot"
But it was only because of their damn plot.

The Song

We arrived on the job at a large grocery store and central heating was being installed – not the thin copper pipes of today, but black iron-threaded pipes, in this case up to four inches in diameter. It came to the morning break and what turned out to be the beginning of many an amusing moment of hilarity.

On this job was a bricklayer who was building a chimney from the sectional boiler which was to fire the heating system. On the concrete yard was a batch of sand and cement waiting to be mixed. I overheard him say, "To mix this batch in this weather," because it was freezing, "it will be frozen solid before I can lay any bricks."

So, being the bright lad I thought I was with a tremendous amount of two hours' experience, I went up to the bricklayer and said, "Hey mate, why don't you mix it with hot water?"

The bricklayer had been talking to the shop girls and shop hands and, as you can imagine, everybody fell about holding their sides – I slunk away.

In the next few weeks it was cut, thread, screw and clip the pipework throughout the building. At that time it was a nine-hour day and a forty-nine-and-a-half-hour week and there was not a lot of time-wasting. Still, for all that, amusing incidents happened: take the time I sang 'Now is the hour' down, or rather up, the pipework.

The sectional boiler was to be installed in the basement and the pipe work was fitted awaiting final connections when the time came, and in the main part of the shop above were the open ends of pipework as the job progressed. This, of course, made an ideal communication system, particularly when break time came. As I was the tea boy, I found that by standing on a wooden box I could speak into the four-inch fitting and shout, "Tea up lads!" And this could be heard very clearly in the shop. It saved tearing about all over the place. The lads had found out that I used to sing in the choir at church and also at school. The school choir won a cup and I came second, singing solo (there was a tie for first place) in the area youth festival, so it can't be bad to take an interest in things can it?

However, this day I was continuously being badgered to sing, and I only agreed on the condition that no customers were in the shop. I sang, as I said before, 'Now is the hour' and, having completed this rendering, I was informed that there was a shop full of customers who would not be served but even if they had been would not leave the shop until I had finished singing. I was told they enjoyed it, but after that I didn't enter the shop for the next two days unless it was clear of customers. I will say this though, the people who worked there were extremely courteous and efficient; it was nice to hear 'please' and 'thank you'. It is a pity these are not heard more today; as the saying goes, 'courtesy costs nothing'.

When people say to me and other plumbers that there is nothing to our job, we quietly agree but on odd occasions they end up with red faces, especially when something goes wrong with their heating or plumbing and that 'nothing to your job' bounces back in their faces. When faced with this situation one carries out the repair and keeps smiling, with courtesy of course.

The Lid

It's only made of tin
Rattle it and it makes a din
It has other uses too
Like a mirror for looking through.

This lid of tin
Was shining bright
Slipped near the legs
Oh! What a sight.

Were they blue or were they white?
This metal lid, had them in sight
If they had looked into the light
I'm sure in fun, they would have took flight.

The Lid

I saw an amusing thing happen one day. Everybody made their daily orders out on a wooden bench or worktop. Then, when the girls were there, one of the lads would place a biscuit tin lid very carefully and quietly to the rear of the girls' heels. You could not see anything as it was all blurred, but what a reception you got when the girls turned round. They all took it in good part and there was no indecency about it. It was very much like the party game where all the men, along with one woman, go into a room and the rest of the women go into another. Six cushions are laid about two-foot square apart and the first lady volunteer is blindfolded and led into the room. She walks along, placing each foot on a cushion, and when she has completed this (walking along to the other side) a man lies between the cushions and looks up towards the ceiling. The lady turns round and the blindfold is removed and, believe me, it is an education to hear the remarks! If you have not tried this you don't know what you are missing! You would end up crying with laughter.

The Mighty Boiler

The mighty sectional boiler
It's made of cast iron you see
Through the years it's stood the test of time
Delivering hot water for home and industry.

It's fed by solid fuel
Processed from the mine
It's built to take the stress and strain
And stand the tests of time.

They used to be hand fed
Then mechanical, that saves time
This powerful boiler, with a glowing fire bed
Producing hot water, through the years of its prime.

These mighty boilers, the best in the time
Needed skills when erecting to keep them sealed and in line
Completion was best, "Fill up and test"
After all that, feeling shattered, you needed the rest.

When up to heat level, its insulation coat applied
Three coats are needed to give it some hide (skin)
The primer and gloss paint its insulation to hide (not seen)
It stood there in its livery to be looked on with pride.

The Mighty Boiler

Incidents happened on the internal scaling of sectional boilers where you worked inside with a pointed hammer gently chipping away the scale, which, of course, if allowed to continue to build up would impair the efficiency of the boiler output. Whilst carrying out this process, your mate who may have been inside the boiler with you, if large enough, would leave, throw in a handful of paper, close the bottom door and, as he was closing the top, would say, "Right, we are going to fire the boiler now!"

This was all part and parcel of the idea of your becoming a man as well as a tradesman. I suppose this is some kind of hereditary occurrence, which has been passed subconsciously down through the centuries as a test of stability, strength and courage, though I doubt if that was what they were thinking at the time. The secret of how to overcome these tactical ways was to show no interest whatsoever, as in this case and just continue descaling by chipping away. This was an easy thing to say when you consider you were fighting fear created by yourself. As you grow older you learn to evaluate other people's actions and thoughts and act accordingly.

After a time these things happened very rarely. Everybody concerned, including myself, took it in good fun because the different tradesmen were not irresponsible idiots - far from it. They knew how far they could go and knew what they should not do. They would have given you the shirts off their backs had you asked them. A lot of them, of course, were ex-servicemen who had been in the war and for whom I had (and still have) tremendous respect. The thing they would not stand for was cheek; it was certain to bring a boot up your rump, a clip around the ear or seven pounds of putty thrown at you - this happened to be my fate once and I am sorry to say it hit me!

The erection of a sectional boiler was a very interesting process to watch; it needed clear thinking as to what you were doing and a great amount of patience. The sections came in various sizes according to the output you required - the larger the boiler the more difficult it was to handle, not only

19

because of the weight but because the waterways were joined together at each section by nipples – no not those kind! They were cast-ground with a slight lead on each side and were placed in the required waterways, which, of course, were machine-ground to suit the nipples. Having done this, and remembering to give them a finishing coat of boiled linseed oil, the next section was lifted onto the base and then your problems really began.

The section had to be exactly in line with each nipple before it could be drawn onto the last section – not as easy as it sounds and it was at a time when plumbers and heating engineers' dearest wish was that all those people who had said things like 'we could do your job' were present so they could take over and we could stand and watch them.

There is a saying which goes, "I have extruded better plumbers than you" to which the reply would be, "Then extrude two more and let us go home". Rude but effective if you know what I mean.

The Plumber

A plumber is of special breed
Whose aqua knowledge is indeed
Required by all our human need.

Yet all too often much maligned
By people who are just too blind
To see the problems there at hand
Put right by this illustrious band.

These men of whom strange tales are told
Of water pouring from wrong holes
Leaking sinks and lavatory bowls
And mysterious bursts in deep dark holes.

Be thankful that such men are here
And wish them well and all good cheer
For if they all were to disappear
The smell and mess wouldn't half be queer.

The Plumber

I remember one job where we were stripping down a boiler to replace some sections. We ran out of nipples and others were cracked on the old sections of the boiler. Anyway, the boss asked me to fetch some as I had a small motorbike. At the time I was delighted because it meant a ride some eighteen miles to the boiler manufacturers. Everything went well; it was a lovely morning with the sun shining and the birds singing and I went pop, pop, popping along and pop, pop, popping back.

On arriving back at the office I let the boss know how I had got on and that I had got all that I had gone for. He said, "Before you get back on the job, nip down to the post office and fetch me a sheet of stamps". This I did, and I parked my motorbike outside. I carefully put the stamps in my pocket, sat astride my machine and proceeded to put it into gear, holding the clutch in and tried to kick start it into action. But, try as I might, it would not start. Now, some ten yards in front of me to my left was a bus stand and a queue of some thirty people was waiting. I, being motorbike mad, decided I'd start the bike like a racing motorcyclist by running alongside the machine with one hand on the clutch and the bike in gear. Then, at the right time, I would jump side-saddle onto the machine and at the same time let out the clutch.

Well, everything seemed to be going according to plan, except by this time I was in front of a grandstand of thirty people. The whole idea of a running start is, of course, to stay on your bike; I did not. Upon launching myself onto it I just kept going, landing in a heap on the other side, and the bloody bike fell on top of me. Unhurt – the bike, incidentally, still not started – I got up as best I could without daring to look at the people and slunk away out of view. I pushed the bike onto its stand and kick started it again and – low and behold – it burst into life. Well, without going into graphic detail, it must have been the motorbike with the longest, strangest name in history.

The Pink Bloomers

We cut a hole out in the floor
The heating pipes to fit
Then we clambered in this hole
With room enough to sit.

One day when we were down the hole
The pipework we were plumbing
We heard some footsteps on the floor
The lady she was coming.

She strode the hole
With no surprize
She'd failed to see two pairs of eyes
Which gladly gazed at pinken thighs.

The eyes the thighs could only see
Pink bloomers masked the rest
I wonder what we would have seen
If she had been undressed.

The Pink Bloomers

I was on one job with a plumber installing domestic central heating, still in the black iron pipe days, and the bottom loop had to be taken beneath the wooden floors. Now you cannot draw lengths of black iron pipe under floors; they have to be cut to suitable lengths, so the procedure was the same as it is today.

The first task was to cut a trap in the wooden floor between the joists, and then survey beneath for parting walls - honeycombed supporting walls for the joists and floor. Now, if you have worked down a mine or been down one, you can imagine some of the problems you encounter. I do not mean millions of tons of rock and coal above you, but I do mean the sheer awkwardness of the situation that you are faced with, before and whilst you are carrying out your job.

This particular job had added hazards, which were clinkers. Great big chunks of them had been used as infill, all over the sub-floor. So you can imagine a hole in the floor which you must first wriggle through and then wriggle under the floor to get into position, to receive a piece of pipe one-and-a-half inches in diameter and about five feet long. Having managed to get the pipe beneath the floor, you set yourself in the direction to which you are working. You must remember that the height under the floor was only something like eighteen inches (this, of course, varied from house to house). So off you set.

The first obstacle would be a brick honeycombed wall which you had previously chopped a hole through with a hammer and chisel. Lying on your tummy or side, whichever way was the easiest, you would worm you way through the obstacle, pulling the pipe and possibly a twenty-four-inch Stillson wrench and chain dogs with you. Then you would crawl, sometimes ripping your knees, arms and face.

If you had to travel on your back, it was one hell of a game and extremely uncomfortable if you crawled over a clinker. Nine times out of ten it planted itself right between your shoulder blades - very painful and exhausting because these jobs went on all day and the next, until the pipework was finished. Needless to say what a job it was.

Having arrived at your destination, you then had to screw the pipe into position. I suppose I was very fortunate to be with a plumber with a sense of humour, who managed to get tears of laughter rolling down my face.

One day we had just got down through the trap. My mate had been joking about above ground, and he let one hell of a raspberry go just as we heard a Lady's footsteps approaching along the floor. It sounded so loud that we thought she was bound to hear it and we burst out laughing. We laughed even more having peered up the hole into the room. Semi-darkness fell as a pair of legs took one stride across the hole. It left a view of the largest pair of pink bloomers you have ever seen, covering thighs that would have crushed you to death I am sure. My mate whispered, "Have you ever seen such pink passion killers in your life?" And being full of laughter we erupted again. Happy days! A plumber without a sense of humour never makes a good plumber, take my word for it.

The Sports Record

I've often loved like most of you
The best is on the bed
We do it for the both of us
And nothing more is said.

To fit a contraceptive
You must really use your head
But to mark down your achievements
With the packets that were red.

Seems a funny thing for anyone
But then it takes all sorts
It was no doubt his record
Of his weekly, nightly sport.

The Sports Record

We went one day to a row of small shops that was once a row of cottages, the ground floors now part of the shops and the upstairs now the living quarters. Well, as a water supply was needed in this particular set of living quarters and the supply was at the back of one of these shops, the task in hand was to make a connection there and to pipe it to the required point upstairs. We piped through the shop and arrived at a point where we needed to pass through the ceiling. Now normally it was best to take the pipes below the floorboards, so if the room had furniture in it you had to juggle the various items out of the way to pull up either a carpet or an oilcloth, which most houses had in those days. Having rolled up the oilcloth, you had to be careful not to tread or fall on it or you would simply split it into pieces. Having finished that particular area and wanted to move to another part of the floor, you had to do it all over again. This became very frustrating at times because you got into a certain rhythm with what you were doing and all that had to stop while you manoeuvred everything around. Fortunately, this was not the case in this job, as the previous occupants had left, and all that remained in the room was an old bed. So it was a simple matter to dismantle this and place it out of the way in readiness to roll up the oilcloth. Well, as we rolled up the oilcloth we found condoms on the floor at the side of bed – and rows and rows of French letter packets laid neatly on the floor.

It reminded me of the Battle of Britain pilots who painted their achievements on the fuselage of their aircraft. But this was an achievement that was kept hidden. I often wondered whether, when he was on his own, he rolled that floor covering back to take a long, loving look at the conquests that he had made. I can just imagine him saying to himself something like, "Second row down, fourth across. "Now that one was a brilliant affair. It really drained my passion" – jammy swine. It's a pity that he couldn't get gifts in exchange for so many packets.

I'll bet he could have bought a car and had the ride of a lifetime,

27

metaphorically speaking of course. It would have been a proper little love machine, but then you don't get gifts, and anyway some would say, "It's like eating a banana with the skin on".

The Gutter

Twas a sunny morn to start it
The rotting gutter lay there
I had to wire-brush it
To lay the metal bare.

My next job was to paint it
With red oxide, brushed with care
And the old man leaning on the wall
Looked on in absent stare.

My next job was to fix it
The best that I knew how
I couldn't have thought at that time
That I'd get in such a row.

My hands were red from painting
My chest was full of pride
I saw the plumber coming
His rage he could not hide.

A verbal rocket followed
My chest of pride was gone
I had to take the lot down
The old man just looked on.

The Gutter

It was about that time of year when we did some maintenance on a row of houses, which entailed every type of repair. I remember the sun shining but it was cold, as happened quite often. Due to various emergencies, the plumber was called away to another job, which would not take too long.

The problem was, what could the apprentice do? There were some outbuildings to this property and to say that the guttering needed repair was an understatement, with some pieces missing altogether. Well, we had saved a lot of gutter, any that might be of some use, from the main building when they had been repaired or renewed, so I was told to clean them down and give them a coat of red oxide, inside and outside. When I'd completed that, if he, the plumber, had not returned I was to start to fix it. To be told to do something like this, especially when you had never done it on your own before, was something that could quite easily go to your head. Especially when, leaning on a wall opposite, was an old man who you instinctively wanted to impress with all your new-found knowledge.

I often wonder what he must have thought of my painting. The gutter was painted all right, but so was I; in fact there was more paint on me then on the gutter. My hands were totally red and very nearly all of the front of my overalls.

"Nasty job, painting," I said to the old man, who nodded I thought in approval, but I probably doubt that now. Next came the installation of the said gutter. Now you are supposed to fasten a bracket at the highest point and one at the other end of the fascia at the lowest point, and fasten a taut line between each one, setting your brackets to that line at the correct distance as you go. I was faced with what I thought was a difficult problem. I've since learnt over the years that if you apply the basic principle to a problem it becomes relatively easy to understand.

Man cannot make or create anything that man cannot understand, only God can do that. However, when you are learning basic principles, in the beginning it does not mean a lot even when you apply common sense.

Common sense can only be applied on what you are told. The English language being what it is, one can understand, or be excused for, some of the clangers that are dropped day to day. I was told, "Fit all the gutter together matching it best you can" and boy I did just that with speed and confidence. Alas, all was wrong as I soon found out when the plumber stepped back on the job.

"What do you think of that?" I said, feeling very proud of myself. The old gentleman was still leaning on the wall in the background. The plumber strode up and then down looking at the gutter which was at about shoulder level.

"Take it all down," he said.

"Why?" I asked.

"Why? Because it is not fitted properly," he replied as he pointed out that I had put four inches in four-and-a-half-inch spigots, four-and-a-half-inch into five-inch socket to socket – all half-round gutter I hasten to add, of course.

After all this had happened and my pride had crashed about my feet, I cleaned my hands in preparation for the next task. Down it came, nut and bolt, length by length, until once again there was more paint on me then on the gutter.

"Now re-fix it and do it properly," I was told in no uncertain terms.

I looked at the old man who I have no doubt had seen it all before at some time in the distant past. He smiled and walked away. I did put it right and in doing so learnt a little bit more about life, like 'pride goeth before a fall' and 'if a job is worth doing, it is worth doing well'.

The Bath

We went up to the bathroom
I followed close behind
And what we saw beyond the door
Was furthest from my mind.

The door was pushed right open
It revealed a lovely sight
The bath contained a maiden
Her shapely body bright.

Apologies were given
She gave a lovely smile
My mate reversed in ecstasy
He'd forgotten me for a while.

He trampled on my boots and toes
I had to stand the pain
But from what I'd seen beyond the door
I'd go through it all again.

32

The Bath

I moved on to another job, with another mate this time. It was an extension to an existing building and was extremely interesting because it covered a lot of different kinds of jobs – the alteration of existing pipework, the extension of the heating system, the lead work on the roof and the glazing.

I remembered working on this large house, as it was then even without the extension. Sometime before, we had been repairing the boiler and having completed that we moved inside as some minor repairs were to be carried out in the upstairs bathroom. Now, staying at this house on various occasions, this being one of them, was the niece of the householder and she was single and gorgeous. Anyway, being an extremely well-mannered breed, if you faulted on good manners you were soon told about it.

"May we attend to the work in the bathroom?" we asked.

Well, unbeknown to us and apparently everyone else, unless the others had forgotten, in the bath soaking herself was the young woman. There are things you see in everyday life that you tend to take for granted and there are others, sometimes fleeting moments, that you never forget – this was one of them, although there was nothing vulgar or degrading about it; more an air of magical mystery surrounded the sight. Off we went up the stairs, myself close on the heels of my mate, in fact like a chicken following a broody hen, as I was once described!

Having gone up the stairs and along the landing, opened the door and then gone down two steps, we found ourselves located some two-thirds along the length of the bath and there amongst the bubbles was one of nature's beauties, but for one moment I thought I was not to see it, for the plumber, being the courteous soul he was (or more probably embarrassed!) tried to back out.

However, as his previous abrupt halt had forced me to do likewise, he crashed into me and almost overbalanced. He did a quarter-turn to the left and, at the same time, a quarter-turn reverse-march all over my feet, which was painful to say the least. There we were, reverse-marching to the foot of

33

the two steps. I was unceremoniously bundled up the stairs and it was then that I saw her. What inward passions a woman can trigger off, for all I could see was a lovely face and the top of two heaving breasts. What mystery lay beneath the water? What was love really like? I was never to know, nor was I ever to ponder on the subject further, for in those few seconds I was up the steps and out of the door and onto the landing. The plumber closed the door saying, "Very sorry dear, I'm so sorry dear".

Closing the door we returned downstairs, crunched feet and all, but she had such a wonderful smile – it was worth it.

The Ladder

The day we did some painting
Upon a hill so high
A force of wind was blowing from
Earth up to the sky.
It whipped across the ladder
And threw it to the ground
How it did not break it
We were struck dumbfound.

You'd better go and see the boss
The tradesman issued orders
And on my bike I cycled off
To tell of our disorders.

I found the man in question
My story blurted out,
I awaited his suggestion
And nearly got a clout.

I could not find the reason
For his non-comformity,
Then fortunately I remembered
I said, "unfortunately".

The Ladder

The whole beauty of this trade is the fact that you are never in the same place long; there is plenty of variety and you certainly never have time to get bored. I am not the type who could work indoors or in one place. They say variety is the spice of life and whoever said it certainly knew what they were talking about.

The jobs came and went, the plumber solving each one completely. We'd move on from beneath a floor to the top of a ladder, from the bottom of a trench to the top of some roof. It was all part of the job, like the time we were sent to paint a very high gable and barge board.

The house was situated on the brow of a hill and the wind was blowing quite strongly and what made it worse was the fact that we were between two detached houses, which funnelled the wind into the gap between. Now, we had ladders erected in this space and the barge board was some forty feet in the air. All this meant we had to climb the ladder to do the job. With paint and brush in one hand and holding on to the ladder with the other, it became rather precarious as you climbed higher, especially if the wind gave a gusty blast. You would climb allowing for the wind hitting you and then suddenly there would be no wind. At these moments your heart was in your mouth as you did not know whether to lean left or right or climb. The best thing was to hold fast until it blew again. You had to have faith in the ladders, which were always tied with a rope and staked at the bottom, but apart from that your mate always stood on the bottom of the ladder to anchor it.

The real danger occurred when you wanted to move the ladder from one position to the next. I am talking about pole ladders here, not extending ladders. Pole ladders are exactly as they sound, basically a large pole tapered off from the base to whatever height you want. It would be fastened together with stays and wire support fasteners, so it was not a question of lowering your ladders to reduce the height; you had it as it was. There were proper ways of lowering and erecting ladders, but if the wind caught them it had different ideas of how to drop a ladder. So was the case for this day, for as we moved the ladder the wind got hold of the top and, whoosh, over she went.

Struggle as we may, we just could not hold it. Crash! The ladder hit the ground. Feverishly, we inspected it for breaks or cracks – everything okay. What a relief. We were sure to get a rocket if it had not been so.

"You had better go and tell the boss that it is too dangerous to work in this wind, so he can give us another job to do until it is calmer," my mate said.

So off I set on my pushbike down to the yard, and there was the boss which was lucky or unlucky according to how you want to look at it. Now, having had a reasonably sound education and having been in an 'A' class, what I was about to say was not in keeping with what I had been taught.

"What's the matter, my boy?" asked the boss.

"Well sir, the wind has blown the ladder down and unfortunately it did not break it."

Silence fell and then eruption as if all hell had been let loose.

"Ladders! Wind!" he bellowed "You've got to have nerves of bloody steel," he continued.

I cowered in silence. What have I said? I wondered.

He continued to bellow, "Get back on that job and don't let me hear anymore about the wind blowing over ladders."

I ran out of the yard as fast as my little legs would go. I can understand what people mean when they say it was like facing a mythical dragon. I'd certainly had my earholes singed that day.

Peddling away back to the job, I was still wondering what had brought on such a barrage when suddenly I realised what I'd said. Oh God, I thought, it should have been "*fortunately* it did not break". I was now faced with telling my mate, and this one was not so understanding. What a day!

On arriving back, the inevitable question was asked – "What did he say?" – so I told him the story.

"Bloody idiot," he responded and made me do most of the work up the ladder for the rest of the day. Still, you live and learn.

The Handicap

It was just the same as other days
Or so we four lads did think
We sat around all munching
And having our hot drink.

We did not see the strategy that had
Been worked out, you see
They guarded all the doorways
There was no way to flee
Our trousers off they wanted
And that was soon to be.

What they saw surprised them
I was the largest see
You're handicapped, they said to me
Next time we will debag three.

The Handicap

Round about this time, shortly after the completion of a heating job, we were sent to a row of cottages in the subsidence area. These types of jobs, of course, had joiners, bricklayers, plumbers and plasterers and at that time of day everybody knew everybody else and if they didn't they soon found out. At school I had been nicknamed by my initials and at work they found a suitable nickname for me. I did not know many of the tradesmen's names, but I did know most of the apprentices.

As the work progressed and time went by, it came to one of the lunch breaks which, unbeknown to the apprentices, was to involve them more than they could imagine. We used to have our meals in a suitable room in the house that we were repairing. This time it was in the front room. With the fire burning nicely, all the men and lads came in with their lunch tins and billy cans of tea and settled down. The door closed and all other points of exit were strategically guarded. Everyone seemed to know what was in store, except us. However, after everyone had finished their food and drink everything was to be revealed to all, literally. There we were, four apprentices, and we were informed that we were to be debagged to see who had the largest tool. One screamed and struggled, but all was laid bare. I am not bragging, but I was told that the next time this happened I was to be handicapped. Every time I pass this row of cottages I think of them as 'Handicap Villas'.

The Load Of Glass

The georgian glass was taken down
On handcart loaded safely
Now take it down the yard my boy
And place it there for safety.

With loading done, the time had come
The truck we pushed weighed like a ton
I thought 'Right then, it won't be fun'
If it gets out of hand, we'll have to run.

You'll have to help I cried in vain
The wheels turned round again and again
Soon it will be too late I cried
Disaster lay before our eyes.

Desperate help was needed, but it was not to be
The wheel it struck a kerbstone
The truck handle flew from me
Now I'm in soup, I thought with disbelieving moan.

The glass was on its maiden flight
The outcome could only be disaster
As each sheet crash landed
My God,it was a sight
Glass here, glass everywhere
And then I saw the 'master.'

The boss appeared from knowhere
It was my fate you see
He jumped out from his vehicle
And headed straight for me

My nervous system folded
And laughter took its place
I couldn't even speak to him
As tears ran down my face.

The Load of Glass

At rare intervals in my life I was subjected to bouts of laughter which totally incapacitated me to say the least. I rolled about in mirthful agony with tears streaming down my face, ribs aching so much I had to hold them in clenched arms - totally uncontrollable. The trouble was, and still is, the outset of these happenings was usually nothing outwardly funny; as it was in this particular case.

We were sent to a roof job, which entailed carefully moving Georgian wired glass out of glazing bars that were fitted into an asbestos roof. This was not quite as straightforward as you might imagine, for certain safety precautions had to be taken. We were safety conscious in those days. Having taken the sheets of glass, which measured something like six feet by two feet, out of the glazing bars, we loaded them upon a cart, for apart from having a cycle we had a number of handcarts as well. We placed the first one down, making sure the handcart was safe by balancing the glass so it did not tip up. Consequently, every other sheet of glass was placed thereon and was carefully surveyed by the boss who came at regular intervals to see us, since we were near the office.

Every time he came he would say, "Be careful of that glass my boy. Take it carefully down to the yard and stack it where it will not get damaged."

Now there was nothing strange or funny about that, but he would say that on every occasion he visited us and when he had gone my mate would keep saying, "Don't break that glass" or "You will if you break it".

I was subjected to this right until the last day. By now the handcart was loaded with some eight to ten sheets of Georgian wired glass and off we set - not as you might imagine with both of us pushing the truck. Oh no, I struggled out onto the road saying, "You will have to help me."

"You'll be all right," my mate said smiling. "And don't tip it up!"

If you have ever pushed a loaded handcart you will know that you are the engine as well as the driver and the brakes. I pushed the truck to what was then an island, which had a slight incline that became a mite more considering I was struggling with a load of glass that I dare not take my eyes off in case the truck swerved round or the wheel hit something.

Matters at this time were not helped by the now grinning plumber saying, "You'll be all right, laddie."

Well, having surmounted that problem I was faced with a long, slight slope which led to the top of a hill, rather steep by now. The truck was rolling quite freely. It was starting to gather speed, which I was counteracting by pulling back with my weight and sliding my feet along the ground. At the same time I was pleading for help that was not forthcoming. What was forthcoming, and it was coming fast, was this hill bordered on both sides by blue brick walls and disappearing beneath a steel bridge, only to appear again as an incline leading out into daylight. By this time I was right on the top of the hill poised for what can only be described as make or break time. I looked at my mate for help; none was to come.

"You'll be all right, you'll manage it," he said.

"I won't, I won't," I pleaded, knowing inwardly that whilst I would do my best I would never hold it back with my meagre weight and height. By this time the truck had passed the point of no return, and the weight was decidedly not in my favour. I was not even frightened (I did not have time to be!). The truck by now was gathering speed – incredibly still no help! I was determined to stay with it as it rolled and slithered. The truck by this time was in control or soon would be. It was going to go where it wanted and at what speed it wanted. It was at this point that I decided to use the only trick I knew or had been shown. That was to manoeuvre the truck's inside wheel into the kerb (by moving the handle the opposite way). Normally this works fine – the wheel rubs along the kerb and acts as a brake and the more pressure you apply to the handles the better the breaking power.

This move on my part, at this time, was to prove disastrous but it was the only choice I had. Fate took over the proceedings. The truck wheel had up to this moment been running into the kerbstones at the side and, while attempting to brake it, it must have hit the edge of a protruding kerbstone.

The handle shot up into the air, taking my hands with it. For a fleeting moment I stood there, hands in the air like a prisoner of war. Crash! Crunch! Squeal! And the glass took off and belly-landed onto the road.

The truck crunched up against the brick wall, its momentum carrying it

44

on. Scrunching and squealing as it rubbed its way onwards, it made sure that any glass that had managed to escape damage was crushed out of all recognition. The truck came to a rest. Silence ensued, but not for long as now I had started to laugh. I could see the funny side of all that had gone before.

"Don't break the glass, handle it carefully, you will if you break it".

There it lay, a shattered mess strewn some twenty yards down a hill. My arms and body had, by this time, turned to rubber and I was on the floor rolling around in laughter, tears streaming down my face and ribs aching with pain from the laughter. I managed to pull myself up the wall using it as a backrest. My laughter continued on and on, tears dropping off the end of my nose and bottom jaw. My neck was wet with tears, and still I laughed. Things were to become even more hilarious as, looking under the bridge and up the hill, I could see the familiar sight of the firm's van. If this had a sobering effect on me it was not noticeable.

The van stopped sharply, and out jumped the boss to be confronted with this horrible mess of shattered glass. Possibly you might think an accident of this kind was excusable. I might agree, but to be also confronted by a youth using a fifteen-foot-high wall as a support while he roared with laughter could be, and was not, excusable. He sallied forth, raining down grammatical phrases, which for the life of me I cannot remember to this day. It only served to make me scream with laughter even more, although I must add it was not really intentional.

Up the hill came a friend of the boss who, seeing what had happened, began to smile. It was my misfortune to see this and the boss to see it as well, for it made me scream even louder than before. I was beyond help. The sack, I thought by now, was inevitable. The boss went away. Whether he was disillusioned or whether he had a true sense of knowing what might have happened I don't know. For he had more intelligence than some people might have credited him with.

Still laughing, although by this time somewhat subdued, we lifted the shattered glass onto the cart and scraped up the remnants as best we could into the gutter, then continued our journey to the yard. We were still laughing, I might add. I found a brush, bucket and shovel and went back to clean up any remaining glass. I missed my morning break that day through laughing and when I finally stopped I went to see the boss to apologise the best way I could. How I avoided being sacked is a mystery to me.

Once again, I looked down this hill with its gaunt blue brick sides, its black tarmac surface road, the dark uninviting entrance beneath a bridge of steel, then a quick twist in the road and out the other side, bordered by the same high brick walls. But this time I was met with a bright skyline – it was a very fine piece of engineering. Its name is very suitable, but should be changed to something like Mirth Road or Truck Glass Lane. Even with the name that it has, if you are ever down that way by chance and you start to smile or laugh, you will know you have passed through one of life's happier days, or should that be traumatic?

Luxury Surprise

We went to take a toilet out
A simple job really
And when it came to half past nine
They asked, "Would you like tea?"

We accepted, used our manners
For we like that don't you see
And then we heard the footsteps
And we thought here comes our tea.
But when the tray was offered
We saw the luxury
Crackers, cheese and biscuits
And steaming cups of tea.

They asked us when our lunch break was
We told them half past twelve
And when that time arrived that day
Our lunch we had to shelve.

Please come down and take your place
The knifes and forks lay gleaming
And on the plate from which we ate
The good food lay there steaming.

But that's not all, no story tall
If we had been there later
We would have had our tea you see
No people could be greater.

Luxury Surprise

Life had to go on, like the job that started with a disaster and ended with a luxury. It happened like this: It was a straightforward job, removing a high-level cistern and the toilet pan, alter the pipework and install a low-down suite. Simple, yes, to a plumber, but I have to turn it into a disaster.

My mate had stripped everything out and had found that the main stop taps did not switch off properly, which meant we could not wipe a joint, as it was a lead supply. So we opened a tap downstairs so that the pressure built up and it came out at a lower level, enabling a joint to be wiped. Now, plumbers being the kinds of souls that they are, did not feel that the customer should be without water whilst the job progressed, so the cistern was fitted and a water connection made. Then the water was switched on again. Fine.

"Do not touch the flushing handle!" my mate said.

I did not touch it, but a few minutes later whilst trying to tidy up in a confined space I fell against it. All hell seemed to be let loose, as three gallons of water went on the rampage.

"Grab a bucket!"

Have you ever tried to catch three gallons of water in a bucket that only holds one-and-a-half gallons? Well, it just cannot be done. There was another bucket full of broken pan and general rubbish that had to fill the gap while I tried to pour what I could down the soil pipe. By this time we had got the lot and frantic mopping up was in order. I am glad to say that none went through the ceiling, but I felt the rough end of my mate's tongue.

What was to follow was beyond the bounds of imagination, for up the stairs came a small boy who said, "Daddy wants to know when you guys have your coffee break?"

"Well," we said, "9.30 a.m.", thinking two mugs of tea would follow. The small boy disappeared down the stairs.

Everyone in the trade brought enough sandwiches, tea, sugar and milk to last the day. At 9.30 a.m. the sound of footsteps was heard ascending the stairs.

"Are you up there?" a voice said.

We went out onto the landing and there stood the owner of the property with a tray in hand which contained two mugs of coffee and one large plate of cream crackers with cheese and butter.

"Thank you," we said in great surprise.

The tray was handed over and the gentleman disappeared. We consumed the tray's contents and, feeling very refreshed, continued.

Soon 12.30 p.m. was approaching; this was our lunchtime. We had just laid down our kit and were preparing to eat what our mothers or wives, whichever was the case, had packed for us, when a voice was heard from the foot of the stairs, calling us down for lunch. Very nice, we thought, it will be warmer down there and probably a bit more comfortable, so off we went.

"You won't need your lunch bags," we were told politely. "Please take your place at the dinner table."

It was a good job that I had been taught at school how to conduct myself at the dinner table, i.e. which knife or fork or spoon to pick up. But to sit at the table with a family in your boiler suit was an uneasy experience. We had a choice of two meals followed by a sweet and then coffee and cigarettes. We were even offered a cooling drink of orange as an alternative. What a day! I omitted to say that mid-morning had seen us receiving two cigarettes to keep us going while the gentleman went out. He promised to bring us some back – we paid for them of course. Having thanked them for the meal, we continued finishing off the work.

Whilst on the landing shortly after dinner I heard the small boy say to his father, "Will the men be staying to tea daddy?"

"If they are still here," he replied.

Very shortly after that we finished and whilst taking the kit away we were given a bag of apples apiece. People in those days gave because they wanted to and did not really want anything in return. Such nice people – I will never forget them.

Then there were the people who, when you had spent all day working in their home, would say when you were leaving at five o'clock, "If I had realised you were staying all day I would have made you a cup of tea."

Well, I suppose it takes all sorts to make up the world we live in.

Cinderella: We Stepped into Another World

Like pantomime, no doubt
And there stood Cinderella
With hessian clothes about.

For they were honest people
Their work they went about
What right have we to ogle
Good Christians there no doubt.

If we must set our standards
Of freedom, truth and love
Then surely these same people
Are blessed from him above.

Cinderella: We Stepped into Another World

On one lot of properties we worked on there was a household that when you passed through the door it was like entering another world. Such a sight is aptly described in the same quarters of the trade as a direct hit, and my God, it makes you wonder how people live like that.

Some people describe these houses as slums, but I've seem a row of houses where most of them could be catagorised under the heading of 'direct hits' and yet intermingled with them were at least three houses where you could have eaten your dinner off the floor, as they say, because they were so clean. But strange phenomena usually occur in these 'direct hits', those of friendliness, godliness and, above all, honesty – things that are probably lacking in some places where you would expect to find them.

Getting back to this particular job, having passed through the door, standing in front of the fireplace was a young woman dressed in a way I can only describe as like Cinderella before she went to the ball.

Her apparel consisted mainly of a hessian skirt with tears and patches. She had slightly tousled hair, a pretty face and I've no doubt she was quite an intelligent person. The work we were to do was to repair a burst pipe under the sink, and everything one touched was covered in grease. It almost turned my mate's stomach over and he seemed loath to touch anything. Funnily enough it never seemed to affect me. I could say that I treat such people as human beings and respect to some degree their way of life. They never looked down on me, so why should I look down on them? If the truth were known, they could well be far cleverer and wiser than I was. Also, I'm given a job to do, I do it to the best of my ability, always.

Having completed the repair, the mother asked if I could repair the outside toilet. I agreed and on entering the toilet (I'll leave you to imagine the sight) I found that the siphon washer required replacement.

"How much will it cost?" she asked, having in mind the poverty they must have been suffering.

I said, "ten bob," showing no signs that this figure was far, far below the true cost, and it was certainly not my intention to embarrass the woman in case she couldn't afford it. Anyway it wanted putting right from a health point of view.

The toilet was now functioning again and the lady said, "I can't pay you now." I wasn't really bothered and I must admit I didn't think she would pay it, but she asked for my address, which I gave her and she said that she would bring it down.

"Okay luv," I said and went away to do my next job.

Now, I lived at that time some three miles away from this house and that day's work was furthest from my mind as I walked down our entry at about five thirty that evening. I had just stepped out of the gate onto the footpath when who should be walking towards me but the lady I've described.

"Hello" I said.

"Hello, I've come to pay my ten bob."

I said, "Thank you very much" and she smiled and turned to walk back home.

It was a six-mile round-trip to pay her bill. Who are we to judge how people choose to live when their basic code of life is what a good society is founded on, unless your tenancy is covered by certain rules and regulations which must be obeyed?

The Cat and the Mouse

I went to tell the virtues
Of heating, with all types
And found that I was cornered
Alone and out of sight.

But the lion is our emblem
And 'lion heart' that I am
For I cut and thrust and jousted
Like the English man I am.

They couldn't understand it
For the mouse was their true play
When it roared out like a lion
They quickly backed away.

Now from this lone arena
The lion just strolled away
Out in the cool and darkened night
To fight another day.

The Cat and the Mouse

When I rose up the ladder into management, I was asked to visit a customer and give them some advice on central heating. It turned out that the customer and his wife were teachers, and after a few minutes I realised that this was to be no ordinary meeting. It developed into a battle of wits,. like some sinister cat and mouse game, only this game had two cats and one mouse. However, they soon found out that the mouse had the cunning of a fox, the roar of a lion and the staying power of some future bionic man, who refused to submit and disintegrate under the pressure of the academic thrusting and jousting which was to take place. Possibly they were frustrated from trying to superimpose themselves upon their classes, day in, day out. Possibly I was one of many who supposedly would surrender and walk away, drained and numbed, like a void within a human shell. But it was not to be!

I went along, was greeted pleasantly at the door and was ushered into a small room off the lounge. A chair was proffered at one side of the table and they took up their positions, side by side. Then, as if by some telepathic signal, battle commenced.

"Tell us something about central heating."

Now normally anyone contemplating central heating has looked into it beforehand and has read quite a bit about it. They would usually wait for you to speak and ask, "What type of fuel were you thinking of? How many radiators?" But not this time.

"Tell us something about central heating" coming from two teachers made me a little suspicious; however, being honest and of good character, and knowing my job, I started to explain, not with any set text that I could read off parrot fashion, like some sort of high-powered salesman. That would never suit me anyway. I gave people the benefit of my experience in the hope of helping them. If they chose to ignore it then that was up to them. It's a free country!

"Central heating is self explanatory," I began.

"Why?" came the reply.

"Because it controls the system and functions from a central point and it feeds the various parts that you require heating, such as the wet system," I replied, dropping in the rarely used term.

"What is a wet system?"

One to me, I thought. "Its got water in it," I said, trying to fight back the laughter and keep a straight face. I almost choked. No response could be seen from the two pairs of eyes that watched me. I sensed two imaginary, very sharp claws waiting to strike.

"Explain a typical heating system."

"What type of fuel?" I quickly replied, which brought an unexpected pause.

"We'll leave that to you," the lady said. They had the uncanny knack of filling in for each other.

"Right, solid fuel," I said. "Well, if we are talking about full central heating with small bore pipes, then each room is measured by length × breadth × height, plus the window area. We will also need to know the types of walls, floor and ceiling, and also the compass direction of each room."

"Why is all this necessary?"

"All these requirements are needed for calculation purposes to determine the amount of heat required for each room and the amount of heat loss."

"We accept that," came the reply.

"Then, having totalled up all the heat requirements in BTU's.."

"What's a BTU?"

"A British thermal unit." (This is no longer used today, since we went metric.)

"What's a British thermal unit?"

My God, I thought, this will go on all night. "A BTU is the amount of heat required to raise the temperature of one pound of water by one degree, e.g. from 39°F to 40°F." I thought, now sort that one out. No comment was forthcoming, so I continued, "Having gathered this information, one must then determine the storage capacity of the hot water cylinder."

"What's that?" was the reply.

"Hell, you would like plenty of hot water, wouldn't you?"

"Oh yes!"

"Having done that, together with the room requirements and pipework, because a pipe is a radiator a boiler is selected that is capable of producing the BTU's required. Also from these calculations a pump size is calculated."

The questions were endless, but I never gave too much away, as I'm not doing now.

"Having selected a boiler size, say a pot type, it would be fired by manufactured fuels as instructed by the manufacturers of the appliance. Your coal merchant can help you a great deal as regards the selection of solid fuel. The fuel must be sound and a double-seal soot door fitted. If an external flue is required then an insulated chimney will be needed. Also very important, is that a proper unrestricted supply of air must be allowed to flow into the room where the boiler is located for combustion purposes and the air changes per hour according to requirements..."

And so it went on, through all the solid fuel appliances, gas, oil and I was even asked about electric storage heaters. We went through background heating, selective heating, gravity heating, in fact the whole works. All this had taken several hours and the only respite I got was a cup of coffee and several cigarettes. The latter I supplied myself.

I finally bade them farewell, walked off to my car and drove away into the dark, cold night, secretly feeling pleased with myself.

Someone once said to me, "You had a good grounding in your job, didn't you?" I did, but needless to say we didn't get any central heating work there. I wasn't sorry.

The Shallow Well (Soft Water)

The soft water cistern, dark and deep
Its beckoning sight gives you the creeps
But the job must go on, the fitting's not cheap
Cannot waste time, have a deadline to meet.

The plumber laid prone with head in well
With mate holding his legs, the idea is swell
"Pass me the grips," came the voice from the well
His mate reached for the grips and gasped, "Oh hell!"

The plumber went head first deep into the well
He disappeared beneath the swell
His mate looked in saying, "I'll be sent to hell"
The plumber surfaced, all was well.

He hauled him out without a doubt
A few choice words were blurted out
His quivering body prevented a clout
The mate turned away comtemplating his rout.

The Shallow Well (Soft Water)

It was another long day when something happened and I, together with a good many more plumbers, have often wondered what the outcome would be if what happened to this plumber ever happened to us.

I'd sent out the plumber with an apprentice to carry out what I called 'sweeping'. For every now and again, particularly when we had a lot of large jobs, the smaller ones tended to accumulate. So as not to disappoint the customer, I had one team 'sweeping up' these jobs. On this occasion it would be about eleven o'clock in the morning when into the office came this plumber, absolutely wet through.

"What the hell has happened to you?"

His teeth chattering, he replied, "Fell in."

"How did you manage that?" I said.

Well, this brings us back to the thoughts or fears of what I said earlier, because when you convert an old-fashioned jack pump and fit an electric pump, the lead suction is reused, providing it is in good condition. The conversion inside the house is quite a straightforward affair, but outside in the cistern it is not quite as easy. For if the cistern is full you have to first pull up the lead suction into the right position to be able to cut it. This in itself is no easy task. I also found that two ordinary sweeping brushes placed either side of the pipe to get it lifted was the best method. Having achieved this, the next thing is to secure it with a rope, which enables you to remove the unwanted piece of lead. You are left with a short piece of inch-and-a-quarter pipe, which can only be reached by lying down on your stomach and reaching into the cistern, and, as you can imagine, it's quite difficult as the lead has to be dressed or worked down in size to receive the connections.

A piece of copper tube three-quarters of an inch smaller than the end of the pipe has to be prepared. Then, with a gas torch in one hand and the metal wiping cloth in the other, you have to wipe the joint. After that it is just a matter of placing the already prepared copper suction pipe, with a

58

foot valve attached, into the cistern and connecting it up with an elbow connector.

Now let's return to the plumber who, having placed the pipe down into the cistern and tightened the nuts on the elbow, half turned his head to speak to his mate. The mate played an important part in this operation, by holding down the plumber's legs so that the man did not slide forward. The plumber asked him to pass the grips, which were just out of reach. The mate moved to get nearer to them and in the process let go of the legs he was holding. Zip – out of sight shot the plumber, straight into the cistern which was usually seven-foot deep. The mate gaped in – stunned with horror – as he realised what he has done. The plumber was nowhere in sight. With heart pounding and wondering whether he should dive in after him, the mate prepared for action just as a head broke the surface, gasping for air and shouting "Pull me out." No true account has been versed as to what was said next, but I'm sure it would have been unprintable!

Having made sure the man was okay, he went home to change his wet clothes and returned to work. It was some time after when the lads were talking that this incident came up and the mate asked,

"What would you have done if your mate hadn't surfaced?"

Very quickly came the reply, "I should have put the bloody lid on quick!"

And everybody fell about laughing.

The Lady and the Rude Word

I called to see a lady
I knocked upon her door
She greeted me with smiles so true
I could not ask for more.

We completed all our business
She asked me in for tea
And showed me all the papering
That she had done with glee.

I looked and said, a fine job
She said I'll get the tea
Her talk was not that of a snob
As she went on merrily.

She began to tell a story
As we gently sipped our tea
About something that had happened
Way back in history.

"This man," she said, "where I once lived
Came along, his advice to give
The conditions were bad, where I did live
And advice was oh so glib.

"On he went without a care
I thought it's time to clear the air
I gave him a boll****** oh so fair"
I almost choked on my tea just there.

I drank my tea and with great strain
I fought back laughter with great pain
I mentioned the papering once again
I then retreated with a goodbye refrain.

The Lady and the Rude Word

I visited a house one day, knocked on the door and was greeted quite amiably by this lady, with no hint of what was to come. I told her who I was and what I had come to see. Once I had sorted out the problem she said, "Would you like some tea?" I said that I would and went into the kitchen. She was decorating the living room with chip-wood paper, and while she was preparing the tea we were chatting about decorating in general and about her decorating.

She came through with the tea and as we sipped it we discussed the advantages of the type of wallpaper she had chosen, the general concensious being that its surface made it easy to redecorate whenever you desired a colour change. It was while she was talking on this subject that she decided to tell me about a set of circumstances that had occurred at her previous address and how a representative from the owners had called to investigate her complaint.

On she went, into every detail, until she became quite animated, like she must have been at that time. For she said, "I got quite mad with him and didn't half give him a right boll***ing."

While she had been talking and telling me of this time I had been taking a sip of tea every now and then. At the point that the word in question was uttered I must have taken a large sip, because it was somewhere in the region of my tonsils when I heard her say it. I almost choked with laughter. How I didn't I'll never know. I just looked up at the decorating and said, "You're making a good job of this, aren't you?" I then drank up, said my farewells and left.

As a late friend of mine would have said, "see what I mean", but then it all comes under the heading of life. Although, on the other hand, it could have been a slip of the tongue. I once knew a respectable lady who was ill in bed and belched in my presence, and the belch pronounced the very same word. It was quite unintentional, even quite amusing, but still very embarrassing, and to show I'm no prude I could just have likely answered, "The usual number mate, ding dong!"

Another Damn Dog

I stood confronted at the gate
By the dog that was growling
"Is it safe?" I asked in good faith
As the dog just kept on snarling.

"You'll be all right, it will not bite
Just ignore it and take no notice"
With this advice I thought was right
I entered, not unnoticed.

The job in hand as I had planned
I discussed at length with the owner
And all this time the canine mind
Was planning a right misnomer.

No, not again, was my refrain
The dog came on just like a train
It bit my thigh the same
And left a throbbing lump of pain.

I yelled with grief and cursed bleat
The farmer called it off
It's used to snapping at cow's feet
I was told through a nervous cough.

The next time it came lunging
The hosepipe it did get
Rammed down its throat so bulging
It almost broke its neck.

Another Damn Dog

We used to do quite a lot of work on farms from time to time. This one involved fitting a new solid fuel cooker with back boiler. Now apart from the weight problem involved in just getting it on the van, we were faced with unloading it onto uneven ground and manoeuvring it over the three steps that led down to the farm. We had to get through this before turning to pass through the back door to get to the kitchen. What a job it turned out to be – having hugged and tugged at one of these, you never felt like doing any more work after that. Now this farmer had a dog just like other farms that no doubt had dogs that would bite you like this one. I'd seen it before running and barking at everyone and I never really trusted it. We had all looked for it on our arrival but it wasn't there. When we got into the kitchen we knew why – it was in there waiting. The farmer said, "It won't hurt you", but having been bitten by a dog several times before, I'm still a bit wary when the owner says that.

I had come to the conclusion that when anybody told me in the future that this dog wouldn't bite, I still wouldn't feel safe. I was bitten as a small boy by a black dog, right on the end of my protruding organ, and I can assure you it was painful. It made one hell of a difference I'm convinced, but that's the only dog I'm ever going to be grateful to!

Anyway, as we moved the appliance across the floor on rollers, I was passed by the dog who decided I was the one who he was going to bite, and bite he did, right on my thigh. "Bloody dog," said I, and it was promptly removed from the room. The work progressed satisfactorily and, as we were leaving, in walked the dog who growled, and I'm sure it was seeking another victim.

He made a jump towards me, but this time his only victim was a mouthful of hosepipe, which was firmly thrust into his jaws as we retreated, closing the door behind us. The farmer thanked us very much and said, "Sorry about the dog biting you." I thought, not half as sorry as I am. "It's used to snapping at the big cows who will clock it one under the jaw," He explained.

The Plug

The toilets full up to the brim
That's when they call the plumbers in
One look and we could see
The patrons had nowhere to pee.

We surveyed to the soil pipe
Upon the outside wall
And soon discovered at one end
A rodding eye to get at soil.

The ladder up, the grips in place
A little turn, no need for haste
Now a trickle of effluent waste
But soon we hoped it would be paste.

As time went by and work progressed
A van rolled up and came to rest
Right in line to catch the mess
If we couldn't drain we'd lose face at best.

The plug was turned to the last thread out
A rushing noise, too late to shout
As a stream of effluent shot out
And gave the van a messy clout.

Soil pipe emptied, toilets fine
I'm glad that van was not mine
For it would reek to heaven all the time
Poor driver, must have muttered, "Filthy swine".

The Plug

We got called out one day to a restaurant which had a row of four toilets situated upstairs. The reason for the urgency was that it was lunchtime and all four toilet pans were full up to the brim. We were ushered upstairs to see for ourselves. What we saw was not for the squeamish or feeble hearted and was probably why the patrons were carefully diverted to other facilities.

"Well, lets get started," said my mate and outside we went.

There, coming out of the wall were four lead soil pipes connected into cast-iron junctions and at the end was a rodding eye. Now in this situation the only chance we had of getting the water level down so we could rod the soil pipe was to remove this plug. We put the ladder up against the wall, which was running parallel to the pavement, and above the wall some ten feet in the air was this plug. Holding the ladder with one hand and a pair of 24-inch adjustable Stillsons in the other, I climbed the ladder. You'll see why I had to climb as the tale unfolds.

Making sure that I was safe on reaching the top, I fitted the Stillsons onto the hexagon nut and pulled down with all my might. It began to move. I proceeded to unscrew it until it was hand tight and as I passed down the Stillsons to my mate, which necessitated my turning round, I noticed that a large van had been parked against the kerb right in line with where we were working.

"We'll have to have that removed," my mate said obviously seeing the disadvantage of it being there.

After an exhausting search, no driver could be found. We had to press on; things must be getting very desperate inside. We imagined a few crossed legs and others putting their legs together whilst holding certain a protrusion which was about all you could do short of tying a knot in it. So back up the ladder I climbed.

"Let it out slowly," my mate said.

This I did, catching the, by this time smelly, liquid in a bucket, but then it stopped. Funny, I thought.

"That's done it – what now?" I said to my mate.

He replied, "Well, there's only one thing for it. Take out the plug."

I gingerly removed the plug and – whoosh it went streaking by me like some gossamer-clad length of oversized sausage. Then – splat! – it hit the van fair and square. It ran down the rain channels down the side, back and windscreen. If anything it had been shot with sh*t.

Anyway, what can you do with a van that looked as if it was ready to go into action in full camouflage, and without a driver at that. We fetched a few buckets of water and swilled it down and swept the gutter. Once the soil pipe was clear,. we re-fixed the cleaning eye plug and returned inside to flush the toilet. Perfect – everything back in working order. "Cheerio" we said, and moved on to the next job.

You know we never did see the driver. I wonder if when he returned and drove away he could smell the effluent and wondered if he'd trodden in some dog excrement? I'll bet he kept stopping every so often to make sure. He may have thought to himself that he was smelling a little richer that day.

Cut Wrist

I did a silly thing one day
Whilst at my work, and not my play
I had a pipe I had to splay
But I did cut it the wrong way.

I paid the price, a slip and twist
For the razor-edged pipe sank into my wrist
I ended up in the doctor's care
He sewed eight stitches for repair.

Cut Wrist

I remember having a disastrous day on one job. We went to take out a high-level cistern and pan, and convert it to a low-down suite. Well, all the old plumbing came out okay, and I tried the new pan, finding that some alterations were required to the earthenware sewer pipe. So I chopped up the floor and removed the sewer pipes down to and including the bend. I tried a new bend that had a much bigger sweep to it and I found that it needed shortening slightly. Now, the only way to take off some of this heavily glazed earthenware pipe is by using a pair of small Stillsons, and if you are very careful it makes quite a good job of it. Today you would use a disc cutter.

But I wasn't to be so fortunate this time. I was holding the bend with my feet and steadying it with my right hand, because I am left-handed. I'd almost completed this operation when a piece came off in the jaws of the Stillsons and two-thirds of it was the glaze only. This is as sharp as a razor blade. Plop, it went, burying itself into my wrist. My mate had been standing behind me but when I turned round he had disappeared. I looked at my wrist and thought to myself, that's a big hole as the skin had dropped away to one side. Fortunately for me, my blood soon clots and a protective blood-clot cover had formed over the top of the wound.

I could hear my mate in the house shouting to the customer, "Have you got a bandage?"

He didn't have any luck, so out he rushed. "Come on, I'll take you to a doctor."

Fortunately he could drive so we jumped into the van and set off. We arrived at one doctor's surgery – not in, the third one in. Three surgeries later, and still no luck, but all credit is due to the receptionist at the forth surgery who fixed a gauze over my wound and bandaged it up.

"We'll try somewhere else," my mate said.

"You won't," I replied. "Take me to the hospital."

This he proceeded to do, but neither of us had any cigarettes and I insisted that we stop at a shop and purchase some.

"Don't worry about my arm," I said. "If I was going to die from loss of blood I'd have been gone long since."

The cigarette tasted good as we speeded on our way. We went to A + E reception and told the whole story.

"Sit there," a nurse said. "We have sent for the doctor."

He arrived within a few minutes. "What have you been doing?" he asked when he looked at my wound, so I told him. "Bring him to the operating theatre," he said to the nurse, and he told me to lie on the table.

As I was lying there, he fitted a small table to the side of the operating table. "I'm going to give you a local anaesthetic."

I was looking at my wound because I was fascinated with what he was going to do, but it wasn't to be.

"Turn your head the other way," the doctor told me, and that was that.

By this time several nurses had gathered around, presumably to see the operation.

If he thought I might faint, he was wrong. I felt some very fine pricks on my arm and then he must have cleaned the wound for I heard him say, "There are the guides".

Then he directed the next statement to me saying, "You're the luckiest man I've seen today. The object that cut you went straight down between the guides. If it had cut them, you wouldn't have been able to use your fingers."

He stitched me up and told the nurse to give me a jab. He went away and a nurse came over and started to undo my flies. Lovely, I thought, can't be bad.

With two buttons to go, she said, "You had better finish that hadn't you?"

Personally it wouldn't have worried me if she had removed my trousers because that's what I had to do. I got off the table and leaned over it. There I was leaning forward with my trousers around my ankles. Jab – one needle in the rump.

"Pull your trousers up. Now you must come back, morning and night, for four days."

This I did, getting some jabs in my bottom and some in my arm. But needles are not bad when a gorgeous bird's jabbing you!

Well, there I was with my arm in a sling and eight stitches in my wrist.

Everybody kept saying, "Wait till you have the stitches out, that will hurt." Fortunately that turned out to be the biggest load of rubbish I'd ever heard, as on visiting the doctor again to have them removed, I never felt a thing.

A big 'thank you' to the doctor and the hospital – you did a marvellous job for which I am very thankful.

Half a Binocular

We had to take the tank out
The lid must be removed
I reached up to remove it
When it twisted and it sloughed.

Then off the top four objects slid
Upon my head they dropped
Then on the floor did skid.

One fur-lined glove, a cover of love
A bino to see, and white knickers free
What a story to tell
But don't ask me.

Half a Binocular

Some years later I was in a way fortunate to have a plumber's mate who was very much older than me and I thought the world of this man. He could joke as well as take one. We had some very happy and amusing times together. One day we went to replace a copper tank, and arriving on the job we took everything upstairs, including the new tank, so we could set up without any hold-ups. He and I had a good understanding. Well, we drained down the old tank and the first thing we usually did then was to take the copper lid off the top of it. I reached up, placed my fingers under the edges and lifted, tilting the lid forward. What happened next was quite out of the ordinary to say the least.

I felt a thud on my head and an object fell to the floor. But that wasn't all – a pair of knickers draped my head next, then I was struck by a fur glove and finally fluttering by my face came the cover of a paperbook. What's all this then? Putting the copper lid down, I discovered that the hard object that had hit me was half a binocular. The book had a very sexy cover. I would have loved to have read what delights the inside of that held. The glove was fur lined and the knickers were white; the elastic in each leg and around the waist had been burnt through with what looked like a cigarette. My mate and I burst out laughing. What on earth could these things have been used for? Possibly whomever they belonged to had had a bird in his room.

My imagination went into overdrive: Having got her in the mood with reading the book he had burst the elastic on her knickers before removing them. He had then tickled her fancy with the fur glove and had had a look at it through the binocular to see what effect it had had, or maybe to see if it was winking at him, or maybe it was wishful thinking on his part?

The job went along even smoother after that, although we burst out laughing every now and then. Having connected the fitting to the tank, we replaced the lid and put all the objects at the back. I wonder if anybody has found them since? Or if any other unfortunate plumber has been hit on the head?

I've often thought he must have been nervous to have been smoking at the time. I think I would have been smoking – not from the cigarette but with passion. Still, it takes all sorts I suppose.

The Trousers

I only answered nature's call
Behind the organ, wind pump tall
We had a bucket that was all
To do our business in.

I went to pull my trousers up
When great big hands descended
And grasped me by the legs and arms
They carried me half upended.

They placed me on the pathway
For all the girls to see
That's the way they came to lunch
From up the factory.

The girls began to wander
Down this tarmacked path
I tried to pull my trousers up
But they kept them at half mast.

"I've got nothing to be ashamed of"
"He's bragging again," they said
I managed to wriggle free of them
And out of sight I fled.

The Trousers

The side roof of the church had to be stripped of its lead, which in turn went away to be recast. Now, stripping away lead is easy, but the relaying and re-fixing is a tremendously skilled job, which must be seen to be believed.

It was at this point that I joined this particular job. The weather was gorgeous, possibly too warm for all the hard work that had to be done. The lead arrived by lorry in large, heavy rolls, which had to be unloaded against the gates at the top of the tarmacked path. The lead was then loaded onto a trolley, which in turn was carefully rolled down the slope to the points where it was required to be hauled on the roof by ropes. Well on this job, on the day that the first lot of recast lead arrived, I was told to get on the roof and assist the rest of the men in pulling the lead rolls up on to the roof.

"You be the anchor man," they said to me.

Due to my inexperience and unseen by anyone, because they had all taken up their positions on the roof, I foolishly tied the rope that was being securely attached to the lead around my waist.

"Take up the slack," came the order. "Take the strain."

By this time, fortunately for me, there was a pile of slack rope at my feet.

"Pull together," prompted the front man and the roll of lead started to rise towards the roof.

"Pull...pause...pull...pause."

This went on until the lead was some six to eight feet off the ground. Then for some unknown reason, at least unknown to me, as I was way back up the roof, the lead slipped back to the floor. Now normally if this had happened, the rope would have slipped back through each man's hands and that would have been that. But due to the fact that they were holding it and the fact that I had got the end tied around me, when the lead hit the floor it of course took the slack up very quickly, causing me to go forward quicker than I would have wished. I really shot down the roof and was fortunately stopped at the bottom by the first man and the fact that there was no longer any strain on the rope.

It was a very frightening experience, which I've never repeated I might add, and I don't know to this day how I missed the rest of the men on my plummet earthwards. It must have been a miracle, for had I crashed into any of them they would have gone down like ninepins.

The lead rolls finally got to the roof, which had been prepared beforehand with staggered wood rolls and had been thoroughly swept and cleared of any obstructions or foreign bodies that could damage the lead. Then came the really hard part – the dressing and bossing into shape of the lead. These skilled tradesmen made it look easier than it really is. They had also asked for blocks of boxwood and from this had carved their own mallets, bossing sticks and dressers, which are the tools required when doing lead work. What tremendous talents a plumber has. Being a plumber is not a job for the dim or weak at heart. It needs plenty of patience and, above all, as I've said previously, a sense of humour.

And I certainly needed my sense of humour at one dinner time when the factory girls were going home for lunch from their place of work, which was situated quite near to where we were working. Quite a few of the girls used the path by the church to get to their homes – nothing unusual about that, except that the only toilet facility we had was a bucket, half full of water, situated behind the electric organ air pump built in the crypt.

Now, this lunchtime I'd gone to do my duty on the bucket and, unbeknown to me, two or three of the lads had spotted me going and had also noticed the girls starting to come down the pathway. So they waited for me to complete my duty and, appearing from around the metal caging surrounding the air pump just as I was about to fasten my belt, they rushed in and grabbed me. They led me out to a position between the crypt door and the footpath, which was obscured by the stonework of the church, which was jutting out at that point. One man watched the girls getting nearer and the other two debagged me, and as quickly as they dropped my trousers, I pulled them up again, getting more infuriated as I knew the girls were getting nearer.

It was all a gag. Before anyone had passed I had managed to fasten everything up and the lads went away laughing. If it had been the girls pulling my trousers off, maybe they would only have had to do it once, or maybe at a mere fifteen years old I would have run for my life – the chance would be a fine thing.

My Heart, My Heart

I said, "I wouldn't do it"
In the wrong I may have been
But what transpired out of it
I wished I could have seen.

The balloon went up with tempers flared
Out on the yard loud voices heard
And those with silent voices stared
While miles away I couldn't have cared.

"My heart! My heart!" a voice was heard
"Feel my heart," her beckoned word
His hand was placed below her breast
A thrill if only 'twas in jest.

A jest, a breast? But who can guess
On Saturday night on the back row, yes
But on a yard for all to see
I wouldn't have cared, nor I bet did he.

My Heart, My Heart

I got into trouble with this customer on one job. It all started when the plumber told me to go down the yard and fetch some materials. It was fifteen minutes before the end of the working day, and it had been a very interesting job. The customer was okay. She gave us plenty of cups of tea. We had installed central heating – the old-fashioned typecompared with what we know today. It had been hard work, but we felt a certain satisfaction on completion, and with everything working all right the customer was satisfied and complimented us, which was nice – a nice compliment, if you feel it was meant, is always good for the ego.

However, the next part of the work was tiling the kitchen. None of the modern adhesives were in use in those days, so it was all sand and cement with tiles soaked in water and walls chipped or scutched to receive cement rendering if it was required. The job was going well and at quarter to five I was told to jump on my bike and collect the materials. I was that annoyed that I said that if it had gone five when I returned I didn't intend to clean up the yard where we'd mixed our sand and cement. When I look back, I realise I was to some extent in the wrong, considering I was being taught a trade, and should have been thankful for it. However, it caused a rumpus and also a laugh, which, to this day still amuses me.

I arrived back after five and was told to clean the yard but, sticking to my guns, I refused. The plumber was blowing his top, and when the woman came in and heard what was going on she also blew her top. I left the room, jumped on my bike and went home. However, my conscience kept prodding me all night and I realised what I would walk into the next morning and, as expected, the following day I got a right pasting from the boss and I suppose I deserved it. I thought, well I won't be going back on that job, but how wrong I was.

Off we set on our bikes and, as every turn of the wheels took us closer to the house, my heart thumped faster as I wondered what I was going to say. I nervously entered the house on our arrival and tried to keep out of the way, which was extremely difficult. I was forced to enter the living room at nine thirty to request that the kettle be put on. I felt totally ashamed, but I've never been someone who is afraid to enter the lion's den. My awkward appearance must have been quite obvious, as I was treated with sympathy. Later on that morning I openly apologised, but unbeknown to me at that time was that when I had left the job the previous night the woman had switched on the outside lights and had seen the mess of sand adjacent to the back door. This didn't help. She burst into hysterics about how she couldn't clean it up in her state of health. By this time my mate was standing at her side and she was saying how it was getting her down. "Feel my heart, feel my heart" she said, and with that she grabbed the plumber's hand and placed it right under her left breast, still saying, "Feel my heart".

I thought that breast feeling was usually reserved for darkened rooms or the back row of the pictures. But then if you happen to be a tit man I suppose any place is suitable, if of course the other party is willing. There's nothing like bringing things out into the open.

The Deep Well (Drinking Water)

There was a deep, dark, dank well
Its use long since had heard the death knell
Its nectared water sweet and pure
No longer became a thirsty lure
Its future was now insecure
For we had come to procure
The suction barrel with lead so pure.

The candle dropped on lengthened string
The flame licked in with light
Down the depth of the well to watery spring
No gas was in the well
Because the light was steady and bright
And down we went and even more
To get each piece we had to saw
By now our throats and lungs were sore
We ascended again to earth's ground floor
No more sweet water to draw and pour
For its lifeline from the well we tore.

The Deep Well (Drinking Water)

One job started, in actual fact, by digging out a trench to lay a water service. The frightening part came later in the deep well, but back to the trenching. I had the oddest man with me and we started to dig. Every time we tried to get the shovel in the ground, we found it impossible. It wasn't rock, but we had no doubt that its clay content wasn't helping and was made worse by the fact that the sun had been shining brightly for some weeks. That in itself makes a change. But the ground was bone hard and it was a case of picking every inch. Sometimes the pick would simply bounce off the ground, so the job wore on and the days seemed endless. At the end of each day you felt as if you had been fifteen rounds in the ring.

Eventually the trench reached the point of entry into the house and then there was more hard material to chop through, mostly foundation bricks and then finally the floor inside. The simple part of the work was laying the copper tubes in the trench. Having done that, before we could backfill, the water board inspector had to be notified, so he could check the work, for instance to ensure that the correct pipe sizes and fittings had been used and that the trench was two feet six inches deep.

Having been inspected, we backfilled the trench and it was while we were doing this that the boss came. He said that we had got to remove the lead suction from the deep well. For those who have never seen a deep well, imagine a circular hole bricked all the way down to a depth of eighty-odd feet. Every so often down these wells are what is called oak staging, comprising oak timbers that are built across the well to support the lead barrel. These become extremely slimy and slippery.

The boss produced from his pocket a candle and a ball of string. He tied the candle to one end of the string and lit it. He then proceeded to lower it slowly down the well. This was a test for black damp, something that all miners knew about. Black damp is a mining term used to describe carbon dioxide, a gas that collects at low levels because it is heavier than air. If you become submerged in it, you will go out like a light, which brings us back to the lighted candle. Fortunately in this case the candle stayed lit. A better method would have been to use a safety lamp.

Now the tricky part came. A ladder had to be lowered down to the first stage and tied with ropes across the top of the well. Then the lightest man went down first and stood on the staging, which wasn't an easy task considering the slimy surface.Then down came the next man, after the staging had been declared sound. The ladder was then tied with a rope to the staging.

The first section could now be sawn into pieces that could be handled easily, usually about six-feet long. Considering the weight of a six-inch barrel, six feet was plenty. These were roped and hauled up the well. This procedure continued until the last staging was reached. Now the atmosphere that surrounded you was cold, dark and dank, the only light being from the hole above. By this time you were standing on the ladder a few inches above the water. When the last piece of lead had gone and all was clear, the long haul back to the surface began, bringing each section of ladder clear and away as you ascended. How thankful and relieved you were when you poked your head out of the top and inhaled fresh air.

Next time you throw money into a wishing well, you wish that you never have to go down one.

The Breaded Pipe

The water would not shut off
The joint could not be wiped
The bread I asked for was needed
To pack the pipe so tight.

"Do you want some food?" she asked
I'll cut you some more bread
I didn't want to eat it
"It's for the job," I said.

"I've never heard of that before
To pack a pipe with bread"
That's why I'm a plumber
With great knowledge in my head.

The Breaded Pipe

There's a well-known saying that goes, "a trick of the trade". I prefer to call these 'tricks' 'gems of experience'. One such gem has got many a plumber out of difficulties. This can only be termed 'breading', a procedure that requires you to ram soft pieces of bread, not crusts, down the lead pipe. It is used in cases where you are unfortunate enough to be working in a house where the stop tap doesn't switch off properly and neither does the last-resort stop tap situated on the boundary. In such situations, if the water flow is too great, the only thing you can do is fetch in the plumber. But if it's just weeping by the valve, then breading is the answer. Having rammed the bread as far down the pipe as possible, the water soaks into the bread, causing it to swell. This forms a very good plug inside the pipe, which enables you to wipe the joint comfortably. Once completed, the water supply can be switched on and the pressure will break up the bread plug. It is then advisable to open the nearest tap to rid the pipe of the pieces of bread.

Now if care is not taken when breading, a most unfortunate thing will happen, like the time I was an apprentice with a plumber and we had to excavate the whole yard to repair several bursts and renew the lead pipe.

Breading was carried out on this supply and the plumber did not ram it down hard enough, and he also put too much heat on the breaded area. Consequently the bread was baked solid and it was seven o'clock at night when the water finally came through and the pressure was not fully restored until the next day.

One lady said, on being asked for bread, "Would you like me to cut you some sandwiches?" Others have said, "Do you want butter on it?" Or "Have you come without your sandwiches?" When they know what it's used for they cannot believe it.

The Walk Out

One wintry day, such a cold, cold day
With snow on the wind, a white carpet lay
It stopped us digging through to midday.

To canvas hut we did retire
A Primus stove was made to fire
The cup of tea did soon appear
This also brought much-needed cheer.

Time went on and snow came down
Our dinner time was running out
Then "Toot! Toot!" A welcome sound
The van had come from out of town.

Jump in lads, you're going now
Until the weather clears
"What luck!" we both said, "wow!"
And wished the driver "Cheers".

Some days passed
Oh! What bad luck
To return so fast
Now I cannot find the stop tap, "blast!"

I'll send my mate to investigate
The stop tap's secret hiding place
While in search, the owner lurched
Along the highway on vehicle perched.

A beckoned wave from innnocent youths

"Where's the stop box," they cried
"Get off my job!", he raged to cowered youth
As on the tractor, he did ride.

"No time I'll pay for hiding
In your hut for half the day"
"Come back!" I shouted in dismay
"Pack the kit we're on our way."

Things I'm sure were sorted out
But was our character still in doubt?
Little did I know in time I'd find out
But when the time came he remembered nowt.

The Walk Out

We did some trenching one day in a field that had been separated into two by a wired fence, and in this fenced-off piece was a cattle trough. In the corner of the other piece of field was another trough and this is where we had to trench from. There were three of us who started this work.

It was wintertime – one of those days that was fine with a wintry sun. The work went well and as the afternoon wore on the boss arrived with a canvas hut with tubular supports for us to have our meals in, and also a small paraffin stove for making some tea. We put our tools in the hut at the end of the day and strapped up the entrance. The next day there were only two of us, a young lad and myself. The day started off as the day before and we set about trenching. Now, in the field bordering ours were the owner and some of his men working with a machine. We didn't take any notice of them, but the owner had been watching us. As lunchtime approached, the weather changed and it started to snow, with flakes as big as half-crowns. Dinner time came and we returned to the hut and closed the doors.

The watchful eyes had seen all this and their dinner time must have overlapped ours. As the time neared the end of our lunch break, I peered out and the snow by this time was falling even harder. Popping my head back in and then having a last warm, we started preparing to return to our digging, as until this was done we could not lay the water service from trough to trough. Then the sound of a motor horn being tooted made us look out and outside was a workman who had been sent by the boss. He saw us peering out and came over the fence. The boss had said "Go and fetch those lads. It's not fit for them to work out in this, so bring them back to the yard". This he did, leaving the hut strapped up, ready for our return. This turned out to be two days later. As before, there in the field bordering ours were the owner and some men, and we pressed on with the job. Dinner time approached and we were left with a short distance of ground to excavate before reaching the trough in use.

After lunch we set about this and we were ready to make a connection to the supply, but we didn't know the exact location of the underground stop tap. Well, unfortunately coming down the road on a tractor were the owner and his men.

"Go and ask him if he knows where the stop tap is," I said.

Over the fence ran the lad waving down the tractor. It stopped and the lad blurted out the message. I could see the owner waving his arms and looking generally annoyed, although I could not make out all that was being said. Then the tractor moved off and out of sight. My mate returned and said that the owner wasn't going to show us where anything was, because we had spent all of one afternoon sitting in our hut just because it was snowing. Obviously he had returned from lunch that day after we had been taken off the job and had decided that he wasn't going to pay us for that half-day.

I had no hesitation. "Pack up the kit," I said. "We're off the job." And off we went.

We walked about two miles into the centre of the nearest town and caught a bus back home. I went immediately to see our boss and told him what had happened, as I knew he would receive a phone call sooner or later. The boss listened and didn't say much. We were sent back the next day to finish the job and we never saw a soul. I never thought much about it after completion.

Then the Praise

Some years went by, I'd been away
Serving my country, I'm proud to say
On that sad day, oh! What a day
"Hi! Where am I going today?" I pray.

I'm sending you back to your mate today
So earn your money, take care in what you say
We arrived on site, with furtive stare
Looking here and looking there
But he was not there, and I couldn't care.

Let's get finished and get away
The job was going well
When round the building he appeared, oh hell!
"Good morning are you well?"

"Yes thanks," my nerves attended
Ready for the rebound boom
Dead and gone, laid the wreath festooned
His heart was clear, malice had no room.

You've worked damn well, and I must say
You're the best man we've had here for many a day
Thank God, he'd forgotten I did pray
But then two years is a long time to be away.

Then the Praise

Some two-and-a-half years later I returned from service with the forces and soon after I returned to work.

I was riding in the van when the boss said, "I'm sending you back to see your mate tomorrow."

"Who's that?" I asked, so he told me.

"You needn't bloody well send me there," I retorted but my protestations were in vain. The job involved fixing an underground burst at the back of a cow shed. I had a young labourer with me and I told him that I wasn't too keen on this bloke we were going to see, due to his attitude in the past. We would get stuck into the job, get it done and walk to the nearest phone to call for pick-up transport.

So round the back of this building we feverishly dug out and exposed the burst. Up until now, we hadn't seen anything of the owner, and I'd just got down to wipe the joint when along the back of the building he came. Now for it, I thought.

"Good morning," he said.

"Morning" I replied, half expecting some comment on my presence.

To my surprise he came out with, "How long have you worked for this firm? I don't remember seeing you before."

So, not letting on too much, I said, "I've just returned from the forces."

"Well you can tell your boss you're the best worker I've ever had sent here."

If only he had known. Well that's life and I've seen plenty of it and heard so many remarks that understanding people.has become one of my hobbies. I know what to say and what not to say within a few minutes of meeting someone new.

The Chimney Pot

Will you fix a chimney pot?
The lady said to me
Of course we will, we'll send the bill
That's how it works you see.

We fetched out the long ladder
We reared it up with glee
We laid the crawler up the roof
So we could have a see.

I touched the pot in question
It stood there dark and still
But the other one behind it
Shot out of sight at will.

It took great clouds of soot with it
The saucepans it did fill
It shrouded the room in darkness
The woman's screams were shrill.

The Chimney Pot

We had just completed a bathroom and the customer said, "While you have your ladders here, would you put a new chimney pot on the stack for me?"

"Yes, certainly," we replied.

We hoisted the ladders up and fixed the crawlers up on the roof, tying both very securely. Up I went to survey the stack. One of the pots was broken. Now, Unbeknown to me, what was about to happen was not going to be very pleasant.

The lady next door had two saucepans of vegetables on the fire inside. Normally this would have deterred me from going any further at this point; however I carried on and reached out with both hands and caught hold of the chimney pot. As soon as I did this - whoosh! The pot behind shot out of sight, just like a rocket, only it was going down. I froze, standing there in silence as I waited for some cry of alarm.

I didn't wait very long before I heard screams of distress from down below. "What the bloody hell is going off?" came drifting up to me on the roof. "Everywhere is covered in soot and my saucepans are full of it as well."

Down the roof I came and made my apologies, but really it was nothing to do with me - it was just one of those things. We helped clean up and I notified the landlord, who accepted my report on what had happened and fitted a new pot, and so everyone and I lived happily ever after.

The Tap

I took a tap off one day
The pressure still was on
It made me count my blessings
For I thought my time had gone.

It hit me in the face full on
It made me gasp for breath
It reduced the glowering manager
To a state of near distress.

He gave me verbal warnings
The water did not hear
For it poured upon the workers' clothes
And everything far and near.
I finally got the tap on
It was such a great relief
I gathered up my bit of kit
And made great steps to leave.

The Tap

I remember having trouble with threads on another occasion. It was quite a simple job really, but to a young apprentice the word simple sometimes led to an unforeseen pitfall, where only experience is the guide. But then it's said that the best way to gain experience is the hard way, or in this case the wet way. Some jobs fall under the heading of 'three minutes, three hours' because if they look easy they invariably are not.

"Take the three-quarter-inch bib tap and replace the old one with it." A piece of cake, I thought. The place where I had to fit it was a small grocery store about three miles from our yard, with a manager and half a dozen men and women, mostly women. So I loaded my cycle and my kit and set off. It was about 2 o'clock in the afternoon as I was pedalling along, which was not easy with a loaded kitbag slung on the handlebars.

On arrival at the shop I dismounted, took off my tools and went to have a look at the job. First I noticed there was no inside stop tap and I had forgotten to bring my stop tap key, which was usually strapped to the crossbar of my cycle. I thought to myself, I don't fancy a six-mile cycle ride just to fetch a stop tap key, which was the key to the whole situation that followed – excuse the pun! if I find the outside tap, I can put my arm down and switch it off, I thought. This I tried but to no avail – blast. Still not wanting to fetch the key, I suddenly had a brainwave. No, a brainstorm would be a better word. I took the tap, hemped it and then put on a jointing compound. I then decided to switch on the tap I was to replace to try to judge the water pressure (now this is a fatal thing to do to say the least). I had no guide whatsoever as to the pressure behind the tap; however, to the uninitiated, a simple thing like water, which we all take for granted, can't be all that powerful can it? Ha! Ha!

Having judged the strength of the pressure and decided it was reasonably low enough to proceed, I placed the tap in such a position on the draining board that I could pick it up quickly, also making sure that it was fully open. I then unscrewed the fitted tap to the last thread. Now, I thought, dummy run. I imagined taking off the old tap, placing it down very quickly, picking up the new one and screwing it into the existing threads, remembering that I'd opened the tap to reduce the pressure. So the dummy run seemed to be just right. Here we go. I grasped the old tap, made a gentle turn to the left – and then all hell broke loose.

My height didn't help because my lower jaw was in line with the outlet of the pipe, and the column of water hit me with such force that it took my breath away. I fumbled for the new tap, grasped it and tried to screw it into the threads. Now as you can imagine, instead of it now rushing at me, the water shot in all the directions of the compass. To the left of the sink was a row of pegs where the employees hung their coats, and water was pouring all over them as well as everything else and running to the floor. To the right of the sink on the other wall was a door leading into the shop and, unfortunately for me, standing in the doorway at this precise moment was the manager.

"What are you doing, boy?" he bellowed (because they all bellow don't they!)

Well I let go of the tap and the water again hit me in the face, making me gasp for breath.

"Stop it," he bellowed. "I-I-I'm t-t-trying t-t-to" I gasped, but it was no use, the water was too strong for me to continue.

I grabbed the old tap and it went into the thread with no trouble at all, but by this time I was soaked to the skin. I could feel water running down my legs into my boots. The manager was saying, "Get this mopped up" and dripping coats still hung on the wall. I seem to remember the odd smirk on one or two of the girls' faces. I cleaned up and wiped the coats down, but I was still faced with the problem of changing the tap.

Some distance down the road lived a chap I knew and he lent me a pair of pliers with which I managed to turn off the outside tap. I cycled five miles home after that episode to get some dry clothes. You live and learn don't you.

The Pipe Thread

The thread on the pipe had rotted
No fittings were at hand
To fetch it meant a bike ride
Through falling snow so grand.

The plumber thought and studied
To solve the job in hand
So as not to send me cycling
Through falling snow so grand.

He said, "Pass me the file"
And he cut the thread by hand
Now there was no need to send me
Through falling snow so grand.

The Pipe Thread

I remember the winter of that year very well. It was very cold and this job really demonstrated the ability of a plumber and also his resourcefulness. We had been sent on our bikes to a farm some seven miles away and it was a terrible day. Snow lay on the ground, there was a biting wind and trying to keep warm was literally impossible. The morning wore on and we came to a point where we required a fitting that we hadn't got. It came as a welcome break when I was told to cycle back to the yard to fetch it. Well, a fourteen-mile bike ride on a cold day works wonders for your circulation. Anyway, having found the required fitting back at the yard. I cycled the seven miles back to the farm. On the way it had started to snow, the flakes being as big as florins.

This particular fitting was required for a ball valve connection in the roof of an outbuilding, and when we dismantled it we found that the thread of the pipework had corroded and simply collapsed. Now there were normally only two steps to be taken. The first was to remove the pipework back to the nearest fitting and then thread another piece of pipe. The second was to remove the pipe back to a joint and convert it to copper. However, in both cases, this was not possible in this situation, as we did not have either the fittings or the stocks and dies. Had I got to cycle back again in bad weather? I wondered. No, thank goodness. "Pass me the small file," said the plumber and he delicately began to file the thread on the end of the pipe, and a very fine job he made of it too. The fitting went on and it was perfect, and as far as I know it's still holding, unnoticed.

The Chrome Fitting

The fitting chromed and shining bright
Arrived all wrapped in tissue white
I signed for it, that was all right
Then into my pocket, out of sight.

I took it out in sunlight bright
It shone like a jewel in the light
I bounced it up and down in hand, my right
I didn't know then what was coming in sight.

A blast from the 'the master' for getting it wrong
My character now was not worth a song
Because I'd had the fitting for far too long
I fully understand the tone of his tongue.

The Chrome Fitting

Thinking of the many things that fall under the heading of 'material possessions', something to be admired by your friends and neighbours, brings me to the time or phase when people wanted something new for the kitchen. The 24" × 18" × 9" white Belfast sink was a desirable acquisition to have fitted, as was required in this job, but it involved quite a bit more than that.

Between the edge of the sink and the back door frame a semi-rotary pump had to be fitted. This entailed taking out the old jack pump, situated over the earthenware sink. Then a hole was chopped out of the wall, the same depth as the new sink, plus 3", and it was about 6" wide. This hole in the wall would be about 4½" deep. Then an 'oak block' was made, usually by a joiner or the local wood yard. It would have a 2"-wide rebate made in the end nearest to the edge of the sink. This rebate ran from the bottom of the block and terminated about 3" from the top, so that the lip went over the top edge of the sink. The block would be tried in position and then removed. Next it was covered in sheet copper with welted edges. Then, along its top elevation, three number holes were made in the copper, distanced equally, to take three taps, for cold soft, cold hard and hot water. Then the copper cover together with the fittings underneath the block would be sent away to be chrome plated and then.returned for the job. Having refitted the chrome parts, the bib taps would be fitted into high-neck extensions. Then the services would be connected below the block. Job done – well not quite!

The delay in completing the work was because there was a fitting missing, which had never been ordered. This fitting needed to be made by brazing two pieces of fittings together. This would also have to be sent away to be chromed. The order was placed, and it was enphasised that it was in urgent need, as the job was stalled until it was fitted.

About three days later, yours truly happened to be in the yard when the delivery of this fitting arrived. I signed for it and then put it in my pocket and promptly forgot about it. Another three days later, I was in the yard workshop. It was a beautiful warm day and I stood against the main doors, contemplating how nice it would be to be anywhere but at work. It was while these thoughts were going through my head that I put my hand in my pocket. Feeling the chromium-plated fitting, I took it out and proceeded to throw it up and down in my hand. As I did so, my boss came around the corner in the van and saw me. He jumped out of the van, ran across to me and gave me the biggest rocketing I have ever had. I stood there totally bemused by his attitude until he mentioned the chrome fitting.

"How long have you had this?" he asked.

"About three days," I said. "I had forgotten about it until today."

"Forgot! Forgot!" (or words to that effect).

"The customer is going spare about it and I'm going spare because it's holding up the job, and also the money."

I apologised, but I was certainly not the 'flavour of the month'.

Many years after, he told the story to a number of my work colleagues. They found it quite funny, and even then I still felt a little embarrassed about it.

The Explosion and the Tea

Not a minute after or before
The tea at three I had to pour
I went to the fireplace, and what I saw
Was a wisp of smoke, the flames no more.

I'd no idea of the trouble in store
With paraffin can, I poured all on
The wisp of smoke had now all gone
And in its place, white clouds rose on.

We'll soon have a fire, my thoughts rolled on
When it went up in a mighty thunderous flash
Which shook the room and spread the ash
Now how on earth am I going to mash?

My heart was thumping, the fire blown out
I was by now left in no doubt
A fire was a must or I'd attract a clout.

But alas by the time
The can of tea was taken out
My mate chastised me, saying it's well past three
How on earth he never clouted me
It's a little bit of life's mystery.

The Explosion and the Tea

I remember working in one village at a small country cottage, where we were installing a bathroom. Now, this man I was working with was a really first-class plumber, and I remember one day he was preparing to fit a lead sink waste, which required a joint. The normal way of wiping a joint is by fitting pipe clamps, when you have prepared the lead pipe of course, but he proceeded to wipe what is known as a rolled joint (which means he didn't have any clamps).

He was wiping these two pieces of lead together by heating the metal using a blowlamp on each side of the joints and then holding the wiping cloth in one hand and rolling the pipe in the other. It was a sight that needed to be seen to be appreciated, and what a fine job he had made of it too. That was a facet of plumbing that's rarely seen. It was late afternoon when he had completed that piece of work and one of my duties was to make the tea, or mash the tea as we say in our part of the world. My mate liked his tea on time – three o'clock precisely. The customer had gone out and she had given us permission to make some tea. In this kitchen, however, was the old-fashioned black lead grate with its boiler on one side and the oven on the other and a smallfire box in the middle with a large wooden mantelpiece and surround. Well, there was plenty of coal on the fire, but I couldn't see any flame, just a wisp of smoke. Possibly, seeing the state of the fire and thinking about the time prompted me to do what I did next.

I fetched the paraffin can and gave the coal a liberal dousing with it. Putting the can down, I watched with amazement as billowing clouds of white gaseous paraffin rose up the chimney, but not for long – Bang! Whoosh! As the gasses ignited, the ornaments on the mantelpiece jumped a foot in the air, and so did I. My heart was pounding with fright, and I'm sure my hair was standing on end too. I was lucky it didn't blow out the fireplace. It produced a flame, which was short lived, and I ended up chopping wood and placing it under the coal, and it took quite some time to liven the coal up before I could put the kettle on. Needless to say, my mate did not get his tea on time – so it was a little frightening in another sort of way.

The Cowboys

They're not the sorts with spurs on
No cowboy hats or boots
Just men dressed up as tradesmen
Who couldn't give two hoots.

The great pretenders that they are
They con and bodge from near and far
No one knows just who they are
So check if your tradesmen are up to par.

The Cowboys

We arrived on one job to fit a couple of radiators and pipework to a small free-standing boiler. Having unloaded all our materials and kit we rolled out the hosepipe and connected it to the drain tap on the boiler. Situated in the corner of the kitchen were the tank and cylinder. Having opened the top door, I could see the stop tap controlling the feed tank so I switched it off and thought no more about it, as we were going to carry out some alterations in there anyway. The hot tap had been turned on and was running merrily. It was only after it had stopped running that we noticed it was taking a long while to drain the cylinder and boiler.

The hosepipe was trickling water as though the system was almost empty, but it couldn't be. I had a quick look around the system and, on checking the airing cupboard, to my horror I discovered that, the idiot who had carried out this work before us had cut off the tee connection where it should have continued up the vent pipe and finished over the tank. As you and I know, water expands when heated, and this pressure is relieved by the expansion tank. If this should become blocked for any reason then the safety valve would blow.

There was another shock in store this day, as no safety valve was found on the system. This, of course, should be fitted as near to the boiler as possible. There are different types of safety valves and various places these can be fitted, but that's another story. A competent plumber or heating engineer will know exactly where to fit them.

As a result of both these findings, the only other way this system could expand was up the cold feed, which was exactly what had been happening. Now, fitted on this feed was a wheel valve; nothing unusual in that, but if that had ever been switched off, it would have resulted in one almighty explosion. We put all this work right and fitted a couple of radiators, which worked perfectly.

The moral of this story is: make sure that the plumber you appoint is a competent man. Contact the Institute of Plumbers for the names of registered plumbers in your area. This will guarantee that you get a good and qualified person to do your work.

The Leaking Tap

When you're over our way
Will you please call in
I've got a bit of trouble
With the tap upon my sink.

It's dripped and dripped for weeks on end
My patience is exhausted
All it needs is you to mend
To make it a good faucet.

The day arrived when I did call
I've stopped the tap, it drips no more
The tap was bashed beyond recall
The hammer she used
Two pounds or more.

The Leaking Tap

"Can you repair a tap for me?" she said, "when you are passing by? It's running but I've stopped it," she added.

Well a few days later we called in to see her.

"It's the cold tap in the kitchen," she said.

There fitted on an enamelled sink unit top were two taps, one recognisable as a hot tap, the remains of the other resembling a piece of modern sculpture.

"What happened to the tap?" I asked.

"It wouldn't stop running," she replied, "so I hit it with the hammer and I kept hitting it until it finally stopped." She stopped it all right! How on earth she didn't chip off any of the enamel from the sink unit top I'll never know.

We fitted a new tap and advised her, next time it leaked, to fetch a plumber before knocking the hell out of the tap.

The Quickness of the Hand Deceives the Eye

I went to help a mate one day
It was at his house you see
With him lived dear old grandma
Who was 83!

We were working in the kitchen
She had made us cups of tea
We didn't even notice
That she'd nipped out for a pee.

Nature called, so off I went
The toilet so to find
The door was slightly open
I didn't know who was behind.

But there on the throne sat grandma
Loo roll in one hand
My trip to the W.C
Hadn't gone quite as planned!

Her knickers around her ankles
Her skirt above her knees
She wasn't bothered about being caught
Only what the eyes could see.

Whipping her skirt down at tremendous speed
She didn't even freeze
I retreated rapidly
But was still bursting for a pee!

The Quickness of the Hand Deceives the Eye

I remember helping a chap out once at his mum's house. He wanted a few alterations done in the plumbing line and I would go round and give him some idea of what was needed. It was while I was there one night that a small but amusing thing happened.

It was a lovely summer's evening and living with them was grandma, who was in her eighties and still very mobile. She will by now have long since passed away, but that night she had got plenty of life in her.

The toilet was situated at the end of the kitchen and entry to it was gained from a door outside. Well, unbeknown to me, grandma had come by us in the kitchen and gone to the toilet and I had felt the need to go as well, so down the yard I went. The toilet door was slightly ajar and so, thinking it was vacant, I rushed in and there sat the old lady on the 'throne' with her skirt above her knees. Her startled expression didn't prevent her from whipping her skirt back over her knees at a speed that would have done credit to today's Concorde. I only hope that if I reach eighty, I'm as quick. I closed the door, muttering my apologies through a wry smile, thinking even if it was there to see, the quickness of the hand had deceived the eye.

It's not all fun and games as you might imagine; most of the time it is a very serious job, requiring concentration and hard work. However, there are the odd occasions, thank goodness, when things happen that give you quite a fright and, of course, others that produce such a wonderful (?) sight.

The Central Heating Pump

The heating job completed
And all was going swell
The boiler was performing
The system heating well.

We left the job contented
To take a well-earned rest
And later on the phone went
It was the client in distress.

Please come along and help me
An airlock we have got
The boiler is singing merrily
But the pipes are just not hot.

I found the trouble quickly
I decided what to do
I disconnected the pump pipework
And let the locked air through.

I bent down to remove the pump
The first nut undid easily
But when I undid the second one
All hell let loose so wildly.

The pump was free, oh dear, dear me
The water just went crazy
There was no time to stand around
Or for feeling just too lazy.

With water hot and air all gone
I'd got to get the pump back on
I held my breath and hoped for luck
That the pump did not get stuck.

On it went, what a relief
I tightened nuts to stop the leak
It was just luck, I do believe
That saved my skin, so to speak.

The Central Heating Pump

One night I received a call from a customer. We had been installing a central heating system for them all day, and before we left we had fired the boiler and everything was working okay so we left. The customer phoned to tell me that they had an airlock and it was causing some problems.

I arrived at the property to find an airlock in a pipe quite close to the boiler. Now, there are several ways to remove an airlock, depending on the circumstances. In this case I chose to remove the pump, which had valves on either side. Taking the pump off would enable me to draw off water at will and would in this case remove the air. I closed the valves and disconnected one side of the pump, which was situated in the space between the boiler and the wall – quite neat and out of the way, but a bitch to get at. However, taking hold of the pump, I started to unscrew the other valve union and to my utter surprise the valve came away with the pump. Whoosh! Bang! A column of water shot across the kitchen and cannoned into the cupboard. That's done it, I thought to myself. (I thought in much stronger terms than that I can assure you!) The customer was hovering in the background, and the water was very hot. It's a good job the boiler was out by now. What the hell am I going to do now?

There was only one option and that was to try to slip the fitting back onto the pipe. Fortunately for me, this worked nine times out of ten. If the cone moved then you were in trouble, so I tightened it up and breathed again.

The Cylinder

"I lit the fire in my house
I'd been away you see
Now it's making funny noises
And it's starting to frighten me."

I wondered what the problem was
As I listened to the noise
Take the fire off, I thought
For danger was there, poised.

I stood against the cylinder
It's frozen was my first thought
When all at once, a loud bang rang out
And a buckled sight I sought.

And there it was – a great big dent
Then another bang as seconds went
It was so smooth where once a dent
For the cylinder was no longer bent.

I tested, checked and fired again
There were no leaks like spitting rain
The miracle had been performed again.

But if you all go out again
Remember, system do please drain
And then remember to fill up the same
Then test for safety, yet again.

The Cylinder

Before going on holiday, the lady had switched off her water, but had left the boiler and domestic water supply filled. She, I suppose not knowing any better, had lit a fire in the boiler on her return and the noise the system was making had frightened her. Unbeknown to her, the system was frozen. She came round to me and told me her story and we immediately rushed around to her home with thoughts of a collapsed cylinder and a few split pipes, but nothing had happened. One of us took the fire off whilst the other rushed upstairs to have a look at the cylinder. Nothing wrong there, I thought as I stood right against it.

Bang! I jumped a foot off the floor as the cylinder just simply caved in. My God, I thought, looking at it in disbelief, I'd heard about it happening and I knew what could cause it, but to actually see it happen makes you jump. As I stood there staring at it, the frozen water in the expansion tank must have thawed out because bang! – it went again.

For the second time my nervous system lifted me off the floor. When I looked at it again, all I could see of the caved cylinder was a slight dent near the area that had collapsed. She was a very lucky lady indeed to get away without any trouble. Now, you are probably wondering what she should have done. Well first of all she should have got one of her family or friends to keep a small fire in. This would have had a twofold effect on the system: one, it would not have frozen up; and two, it would have kept the rooms nicely aired. The other thing she could have done would have been to contact her nearest plumber and arrange for him to drain down the system before she left and fill it up on her return. Either of the two would have left her mind contented whilst she was on holiday. It's not a bad thing to have the system drained down if you are going away for any length of time whatever the time of year.

Electric Shock

In a darkened bathroom
The plumber struggling fair
Cramped behind a bath head
Connecting pipes just there.

His attitude was moanful
To be expected there
For every time he touched a pipe
A tickle did occur.

"I'm sure I'm getting a shock," he said
"The imagination's in your head"
But no, he's right, there are coloured lights
Dancing on pipework, blue, white and red.

Electric Shock

There was a time when we were connecting up a bath. It was wintertime and the light soon began to fade in the afternoon. Even with the electric light on in this small room, it didn't help very much at ground level and under a bath. Well, I'd been doing one or two small jobs when I happened to be passing this room and there lay my mate, half under the bath, struggling as is usual in these cases, to connect the pipework.

"I keep getting a strange tingling feeling," he said, "just like pins and needles. I think the pipework is alive!"

"You're imagining it" I replied, as it wasn't even connected to anything and it terminated at the tank in the airing cupboard, which was at the end of the bath, and even that connection wasn't made to the ball valve tail. "I'll carry on," I said.

As I passed by the airing cupboard I noticed that every time he moved the pipes he was working on a connector kept hitting the tail of the ball valve. I also noticed blue and orange sparks jumping off it.

I shouted to my mate, "You were right about the pipes being alive. You should see the pretty sparks dancing on this ball valve tail." He shot out from under the bath like his rear piece was on fire.

We called in an electrician and he put it right. I think it was running to earth and our pipework was touching it. Although the electrician had given the okay, my mate still approached the pipes very gingerly until he was sure for himself that everything was all right.

Thank goodness everything today is done to a high standard within the regulations, which cover the bonding to earth on all pipework.

Burnt Thumb

I placed my hands beneath the floor
I'd done it many times before
This time I got a shock for sure
It burnt my thumb and it was sore.

I was rubbing down a wall one day
With nothing less than a damp cloth, I pray
And received a shock from the wall, I'll say
I remember the experience to this day.

"Would you give me a hand?" the sparky did say
"Of course I will, it will make my day"
"Switch off the power", the lady led the way
She showed me the switches all on display.

"Disconnect that plug and remove it away
Then part the wires, just the red and black'll be okay"
I grabbed the wires, and let out a loud bray
"The wiring's alive", as I forcefully yanked my hand away.

A voice from downstairs called, "Are you all right?
I've shown you the wrong switches,"
I thought, that's not very bright
So I switched them off and got it right
She said she was sorry, and well she might.

Burnt Thumb

I've had one or two electric shocks in the past as well, Once on a central heating job, which was quite a large one. It was a very interesting job too. We were getting on very well and had got to a small room upstairs.

I was working away merrily, taking up the floorboards ready for the pipe run to be put in. All was prepared and I was on my way upstairs, so it meant pushing the pipe through one end then reaching under the floor as far as I could, grabbing the pipe and pulling it forward so it did not dig into the ceiling. It started to come through very well, till I could, half-bending, pull it up. Well, unbeknown to me, there was a conduit pipe running across the line of my length of pipe. As I pulled up, it touched it and electricity touched me. It made my hair stand up – and quite a few other things too. I sank back to the wall and, thank goodness, the pipe fell away. I crouched there almost stunned into silence.

When I finally managed to say something, it was to shout to the two lads I had with me, who were working downstairs, to come up and help me, not that I needed any by that time! All that could be seen was a burn on my thumb. I'd even caught a belt off the wall while I was rubbing it down with a damp cloth, but the socket out shocked them all.

On another occasion, I had lent my services to an electrician – a simple job, fitting a plug in a bedroom and isolating another.

"Go downstairs and ask the lady where the switch and meter box are, then switch it off," he said.

The lady showed me a wooden cupboard just below ceiling level, which contained switches. Off they went with a quick flip of the wrist, and back upstairs I went.

"Is it off?" the boss asked. "Yes," I replied.

"Okay then, take that old plug to bits and part the red and black wires while I fix this new plug."

Out came the screws holding the wires and the wood screws, releasing the whole of the plug. Now all this time I'd used the screwdriver without touching the metal part. I placed the screwdriver on the floor and reached for the black and red wires.

"Bingo!" I yelled at the top of my voice as two hundred and fifty volts shook hands with me!

I managed to yank my hands free. and a voice called from downstairs," Are you all right?" She was sorry, but not half as sorry as me.

The Floating Mass

She crossed the open courtyard
Where open sewers entwined
She pulled the chain to freedom
It was furthest from her mind.

For she'd launched a great big object
That was like a blooming mine
It bobbled on the surface
Thank God, we're not at sea
For it would have sunk a battleship
And caused a mystery.

The Floating Mass

Very few of you will have been fortunate or unfortunate enough to have seen manholes full to the top. Most people will flush the toilet and that will be the end of that. If you can imagine a hole twenty-four inches by eighteen inches loaded to the brim with what I could only describe as some forsaken witches' brew. This could well at any given time consist of anything edible, digested or otherwise and any apparel used on the lower parts of the body, together with a smell of its own.

If you ever fell in it, that would be the end of you. The order came to break it all out and re-lay the drainage system. The large hammers and picks were brought and the task commenced. Bang, thud, crash all day long until finally all the runs of the system were uncovered, then dig, dig and dig until the drainpipes saw daylight. Some were broken and some had back falls. We took them out, remembering that these pipes were still loaded with effluent. What we were left with were trenches half full of sewage, which was unfortunate if you were unlucky enough to have to go into the trench. Eventually the pipes entering the main sewer were cleared and all the trenches were flushed and disinfected and everywhere became sweet again. However, it was while the trenches were full that a very funny thing happened. It still makes me laugh to this day.

There were quite a few girls working at this particular place and it was decided, in the best interests of all, that the manager should be asked to tell everyone that if they wished to use the toilets, which were situated down one side of the yard, they were not to pull the chain. Well, there is always one, and here she came trotting down the edge of the yard and into the toilets. Now, to some extent I must defend this very nice-looking woman, who, having seen the sight that befell her eyes as she came out of the building, could, I feel, be excused for wanting to flush away everything with clean water. However, what she flushed away was unbelievable. She had, by the time it reached sunlight, disappeared into the building but there was a darkish brown length of stool, I would guess about eight inches long, that looked like some sort of menacing mini-submarine. In fact, if it had been armed with torpedoes, it could have crept up on anyone's ship and blown it out of sight.

How she managed to launch it was a mystery and probably a very painful experience. It was the centre of interest to all as it glided masterfully down the trench, sweeping all aside until it finally came to rest at a bottleneck that had not yet been cleared. Poor girl. I've often wondered if she ever gave birth and whether it was any easier than that – who knows?

I've had a Go Myself

Upon the door a knock came
One dark and wintry night
And standing there before me
Was a man so full of plight.

"Can you come and help me?
I've got a right old burst
I've tried to stop the water, see
It's made it even worse."

Along I went with good intent
To seal a pipe that nature had rent
In a dark, damp hovel, an open vent
Where icy blasts were winter sent.

And when I saw his vain attempt
I understood just what he meant
He'd neither the skill nor equipment
To cope with the frozen open rent.

The solder hung like candle fat
The waters still switched on
I've got to get this job done
For the time is running on.

I switched the water off at once
The pipe I thawed with a blow lamp
A joint so true, you'd have liked it too
With metal, cloth, and know-how-to.

I've Had a Go Myself

I was peacefully sitting at home one winter's night when there was a knock on the door. My mother answered it.

"There's a gentleman to see you," she said. I went to the door and there stood a man.

"I'm in a bit of a mess," he said.

"What's the problem?"

"Well, I have a burst pipe in one of the outhouses and I've tried to solder it, but cannot make it stick on the pipe. Would you come and have a look at it?"

Reluctantly I agreed, not really wishing to leave the warmth of our living room and the wireless – very few people had televisions in those days. Off I trudged up the road; it was only about a couple of hundred yards. I took with me a blow lamp and a few tools, including my wiping cloths.

"It's just in there," he said,. pausing before he turned and disappeared into the dark.

"Where are you?" I asked.

"Just a minute," came the reply.

"I've got a light somewhere."

I heard the jingle of a hurricane lamp as he tried to light it. There was a flash of light and the hurricane lamp issued forth its light to reveal a room, which had not been used for some time. In one corner was a lead supply type and the first thing I noticed was a flash of silver as the light caught a mound of solder. I can only describe this as like I've seen on the side and base of a candle which has been left burning and the wax has set as it has run down. The next thing I noticed there was was no internal tap. Now I was beginning to see why I'd been asked to come.

"Have you switched off the supply?" I asked.

"No," he said, "I just hammered the lead where it had swollen and it burst so I tried to solder it."

My God, he certainly had. Taking the lantern, we searched for the mains stop tap on the boundary of the property, and fortunately we found it. However, it was a square-topped stop tap, so I had to return home for a key to switch it off

Now, an underground stop tap can be a plumber's nightmare if it hasn't been used for a long period of time, because it gets corroded and very often immovable. There are certain things you can do to try to ease it, but the crunch comes when you try to turn it and you can bet this situation often occurs at times outside working hours. Then it's a case of fetching out the water board, as at this particular time it was attached to the local council.

Anyway, this stop tap switched off okay, but before the burst could be repaired all the water in the pipe had to be removed. This in a lot of cases isn't as easy as it may sound. However, this being done, I knocked off the lump of solder and cleaned up the split in the pipe and prepared the surface. I tallowed it and wiped an upright joint.

The owner was very pleased and I left him with this advice, "In future, don't attempt to meddle with things you don't understand. Fetch in a professional to deal with it."

I think that's even more important today with the technical advances that have been made and are still being made. I'd also like to say watch out for cowboys, as we call them in the trade. They are boys who set up shop and really don't know what they are about. Go and see a well-known firm or ask about them. Check with the plumbing associations and for goodness' sake, if it is a largish job, get an estimate in writing. I've always held by the saying, "If a job's worth doing, it's worth doing well".

A Piece of Putty

I've glazed that many windows
With putty from a tin
I've bedded, tacked and pointed
It must be many thousands in.

But when I went to one old dear
The glass she had there ready
And when I asked for putty too
She said, "Can you get it ready?"

A ball of chalk and linseed oil
The old dear fetched for me
"You do know how to mix it?"
Came her hopeful plea.

"Of course I do," I said so bright
I mixed the lot, a sticky sight
But in the end it turned out right
I'm now that lady's shining light.

A Piece of Putty

I arrived home one night and a message was awaiting me: 'Could you call round and glaze a piece of glass in a pantry. We have all the materials'. Having had my evening meal and a short rest, I went round.

"Good evening," I said, "I'm the chap who has come to put the glass in."

"Oh yes, here's the glass." I was shown the window. No trouble, I thought, getting out my rule and glass cutter. Measure, measure, zip, zip, glass cut, hacked out the old putty, tried glass, all okay.

"Would you like a cup of tea?"

Well, very few plumbers I know dislike tea, so I was invited in, sat down and enjoyed my tea. Whilst placing the cup upon the table I asked, "Have you any putty?" For, whilst I am willing to help people in a bit of a mess, I was rather anxious to get home because nine hours' work each day, not including travelling to and from work, made a week seem like all bed and work and no play.

"This way lad," she said, taking me into the now darkening kitchen.

I thought, I won't be long now. Well, have you ever had the feeling that the clock has been turned back one hundred years. That is just how I felt when I was handed a large ball of chalk and a bottle of linseed oil.

"You know how to make putty?" she queried.

"Yes," I replied, somewhat sarcastically, for whilst I knew the principle and its ingredients I was used to getting it out of a drum, ready mixed.

"You will be all right," she said.

Lighting a candle I thought, I've got to be all right, otherwise I will be here all night. I proceeded to break the chalk down into small lumps, then pulverised them into powder. After much sweating and gnashing of teeth, I managed to get the required amount of chalk powder. Now came the messy bit – the mixing of the linseed oil. This was a question of trial and error. By that I mean if you mixed too much chalk with the oil you would end up with some very dry putty or a poor excuse for putty, and conversely, it would be too soggy. So I ended up once of twice with hands twice their size, laden with a partly mixed compound. By candlelight you can imagine how it felt. You have got to imagine as I dare not print it! However, slowly but surely a substance resembling putty started to take shape and finally the completed compound was ready. Hand made, I thought.

All the tension had gone and feeling quite pleased with myself, I said to her, "It's made a wonderful lump of putty."

"Oh, I am pleased," she said. "It is better when you can make your own things isn't it?"

I felt even prouder and thought, if only I could stamp on it 'made in england by hand'. The remainder of the job was straightforward – run the joints, which I had learnt to do with both hands, bed the glass, pin and point up and cut back the putty.

"Goodnight," I said, walking down the entry thinking, oh we do see life, don't we?

The term 'running putty with your hands' is not as simple as you might think and to be able to do it with both hands either takes one hell of a long time or it comes naturally. I discovered that the latter applied to me, quite by accident. I had been working on a new factory that had more glass on it than I would care to recall. I'd managed to achieve putty running with my left hand quite well – I'm a natural left-hander, but I'd never tried it with my right. On this job was a plumber who, from time to time, would quite openly try to make you look like a person who didn't know anything and was not likely to learn anything. You meet all kinds. This day was to be his downfall, because usually on these occasions you have an audience and this day was no different.

Getting two lumps of putty, one in each hand, he said, "Now lad, wait until you can do it like this, then you can call yourself a plumber."

Well, not being the sort of chap that is overawed by anything, I replied "What like this?" Not wishing to be outgunned and taking my meagre experience in my hands, I grabbed two lumps of putty, placed one in each hand, took a deep breath and with all eyes watching me proceeded to run putty into two rebated casements, one left, one right. Managing to pull it off surprised even me, let alone anyone else, but I smiled and thought, that's one in the eye for you mate. I never did hit it off with him.

The Underground Burst

We went to a burst underground one day
There were three of us, let's pray
All goes right, come what may
If it doesn't, all three will pay.

Our teacher came to see us
Which one will get it right?
We prayed for darkness of the night
When we would be gone out of sight.

I had drawn the short straw
It was to be my task
Please get it right, I could only ask
Then in the limelight I could bask.

The Underground Burst

I remember being sent to a tent-hire firm, together with two other apprentices, to dig out and repair an underground burst. Well, the boss dropped us off with all the kit and we started digging out the hole and bailing out the water. We never switched off the supply until it became impossible to cope with the water filling the trench. This was to give the customers time to fill their kettles, etc, so no one would come running wanting water.

It was while we were carrying out our work that one of the lads said, "You do know that our night school teacher works here?"

Now, our technical teacher knew his plumbing upside down and inside out; in fact he was quite brilliant. He passed away some time after this job, and he was sadly missed. I have written in one of my old technical books, in which we used to make notes, a memorial page depicting a cross with his name around it. I'm sure his family missed him and I can assure you that I did. I very often think about him. You have to honour and respect, even posthumously, people who are masters of their profession and, of course, who always take an interest in everything.

However, back to the burst. Having completed the trench, making sure that we had left sufficient room to work, between us we prepared the lead pipe where the burst was. We then fitted the pipe clamps, put the solder and wiping cloths within easy reach, making sure we didn't get sludge on them, and lit the blow lamp. The plan was for everybody to wipe the joint, that is until our night teacher was spotted walking down the firm's driveway towards us. Then the nerves started to jingle.

"You wipe the joint."

"No! You wipe the joint."

"No! I'll help."

I made the following statement, "Well one of us must do it or we will be here all day."

"You do it then," was the cry.

By this time the person in question was at the top of the trench. I've no doubt he could hear, as he was approaching, what was being said.

"Well," he chimed, "which one of you is going to wipe that joint?"

The other two pointed to me. Why can't I keep my mouth shut? I thought. I also thought, into the valley of death again.

So I dropped into the trench, did my best to switch off from those around me and concentrated on the task in hand. I'm pleased to say that everything worked out okay. We backfilled the trench, having first switched the water back on, and then phoned for our transport.

What's that saying in management?

'When the going gets tough, the tough get going!' I wonder who makes up these sayings?

The Pan

As the WC pan was unloaded off the van
It caught the rays of the midday sun
And the passers-by seemed to cast their eyes
Denying them some fun.

But two factory girls who were full of glee
Shouted "Oh! We could do with a pee"
I offered the pan, but the boss saw me
And ushered us away to obscurity
I never did see those girls having a pee
On the shining white 's' trap pan.

134

The Pan

People do things in the company of others that they would never do on their own. Like the day the boss came into the yard just before dinnertime when another lad and I were there.

"Fetch an 's' trap WC pan" he said, "and the materials for fixing."

With the materials loaded on the van, the three of us set off on a short journey to the centre of town and then stopped. The boss jumped out, followed by me.

"Round to rear of the van," he said, flinging the doors open and grabbing the white WC pan.

It was a brilliant shining day with people milling everywhere. The sun not only brings out the flowers, but it also brings out the birds (i.e. the factory girls), and there were three of them walking diagonally across the road.

As they drew level with the WC pan, one of the girls in a clear voice that everyone could hear said, "I could do with a pee"

This, of course, made me and the other lad burst out laughing. The boss did not see the funny side of things, or if he did, he was keeping it to himself.

"Follow me," he retorted, and we disappeared down the entry.

That was the end of that. You never know, it might have been the beginning of a beautiful friendship. It is funny, but I find in plumbing that you get what I can only describe as 'a run' on various jobs like WC pans and drains.

The Washbasin

One day I went on maintenance
It was at a farmhouse old
"The cistern is not flushing"
That's what the farmer told.

He left me on my lonesome
The job almost complete
When I dropped my steel handgrips
Right down between my feet.

They fell into the toilet
The trap it split complete
And the water drained away from it
It disappeared a treat.

I had to get a new one
I fitted it complete
I cleaned up all the mess I'd made
And headed for the street.

I'd almost cleared the building
When someone spoke to me
Said, "You should have broken the washbasin"
He'd been to look you see.

The Washbasin

I remember being out on my own, carrying out some repairs at a farm. I was re-fixing cattle drinking bowls, which was an awkward job at the best of times, as most of the older types of cowsheds were constructed from stone, and so making holes through the stonework to take the bolts was a very awkward process. However, it was the only way, for if a cow got its horns under them it would have them off within the wink of an eye – such strong animals.

Having overcome that problem, there was now some work to carry out inside the farmhouse, repairing the high-level cistern and fitting a new ballcock in the upstairs bathroom. I carried out these repairs, and then, from a small pair of steps, I peered over the top of the cistern to watch the water level to see if any adjustment was necessary to the ball valve. I was holding the sides of the cistern with each hand, and in my left hand I was holding a small pair of grips. I was so engrossed in watching the water rise that I loosened the grip of my left hand and out shot the grips. Now, I'd forgotten a very simple rule, which is – if the seat has a flap, put it down to cover the opening of the toilet pan.

Down shot the grips and they didn't just stop at cracking the pan, they completely ripped out the bottom of the trap. As we all know, there is a water seal in this trap to prevent the smell from the sewerage system getting filtered up through the pan. The seal,according to the type of pan, usually holds two to three pints of water. Well, I looked down and to my dismay there, staring up at me, was a gaping hole and no water. Oh no! I thought, imagining water dripping from the ceiling into the living room downstairs and at any minute someone screaming "Come quick, there is water coming through the ceiling," but silence prevailed. So I thought, let sleeping dogs lie.

I need not have worried. It was an old farmhouse and, although it had wooden floors, the amount of material that was used on the ceiling had adequately soaked up the water. But now I was faced with fitting a new pan and explaining why. I jumped on my bike – no one seemed to be about – and raced down to the stores at the yard and selected a new pan, which was almost identical. At that time you had a far greater choice of materials than you have got today as regards WC pans. Plumbing materials back then differed in so many ways it was unbelievable – that even applies today.

Well, not wishing to ride through the town holding the handlebars with one hand and a gleaming white toilet pan in the other, I searched round and found a sack bag. Stuffing the pan in, I jumped on my bike and sped back with haste. There was still no one about. I quickly removed the old pan, placed the broken contents in the sack and fitted the new one.

However, unbeknown to me, the farmer had been in the bathroom and had seen what had happened, for he said when I was leaving, "Cheerio, and you might have broken the cracked washbasin as you passed." (This was a tenant farm.)

With a red face I hurried off to inform the boss of the error of my ways. A lecture followed on 'thought and care.' He had a saying, which is very true and I will never forget it: 'Half an hour's thought is better than a whole day's cock-up', or words to that effect.

We did all sorts of jobs in those days, which was a credit to be shared with the boss who found work for the men, which wasn't an easy task, and credit to the tradesmen who had the capabilities to carry it out.

The Wrong House

I was working at a house one day
The job was just spot on
The tank was in position
But all the fittings had gone!

I jumped into my car
And to the yard did hurry
Fittings claimed, I shot right back
I didn't stop to worry.

Out the car and up the stairs
It seemed to work quite well
I hadn't been a minute
I bet no one would tell.

But wait! What's this? Something amiss!
The door was the same colour!
But in my rush I'd gone next door
This could get me in some bother.

I crept back out and closed the door
Sweat pouring from my brow
If anyone had seen me
What the hell would I do now?

But luck was on my side that day
There was not a soul in sight
So I just strolled in and up the stairs
At last I'd got it right!

The Wrong House

I often wonder what might have happened to my reputation. One day I was working away merrily at this particular house, when I got to the stage where I required some more materials. So I jumped in the car and drove off to the yard, collected what I wanted and shot back again.

Now this had, to some extent, delayed my completion of this work, as I wanted to finish that day and it was by now mid-afternoon. As I turned the car into the street where I was working, I was mentally calculating that I could still finish on time. I pulled up outside the house, the front door being open as it was a lovely, warm afternoon. I opened the boot, scooped up all the fittings I wanted and ran through the gate and straight up the stairs into the bathroom. I stopped two paces inside the door. Funny, I thought, I don't remember being in this room before. Even the decor was different. Then it suddenly dawned on me – I was in the wrong house!

What am I going to say if anybody comes out of the rooms and asks me what I am doing? I turned round and descended the stairs – still no challenge. I was now outside the front door and wondering how I could have made such a mistake, when I realised that both houses were positioned the same, both were the same colour and both had their front doors open, and I'd simply chosen the wrong one.

It just shows how easy it is to find yourself in the wrong place with no excuse why you're there. But, then again, some gorgeous female, who probably couldn't believe her luck, might have whipped me into the nearest bedroom – I should be so lucky!

Well, that's life. Next time you set foot outside, take notice of what's
going on around you, except when you're driving, of course, because a
little bit of pink thigh or glint of knickers in your eyes could cause a crash
and you could die. So keep such visions from your eyes. Maybe what
you're looking for will still kill you, if you have too much of it.
You should be so lucky? Shouldn't we all.